DARE, DREAM, DISCOVER

FROM THE US AIR FORCE TO THE

MIDDLE EAST AND BEYOND

Jayme C. Harris is a 35-year old successful managing partner for a business firm in Dubai, UAE, located in the Middle East. Growing up in Florida, she was forced to provide for her well being and safety at an early age.

In 1990, Jayme served active duty in the US Air Force and spent 11yrs at Eglin Air Force Base, Florida. Hungry for adventure, she quit her job to work in Kosovo after which she left to Iraq. Jayme was just miles away at the time the US Military captured Saddam Hussain in Tikrit. She frequently travels into Iraq to secure government contracts and support the US Military in rebuilding the country. She still manages and consults for a contract firm for US Government contracts in Iraq, Unity Logistics and Security Services. She also formed an exclusive luxury real estate firm in Dubai, Elite International Investments, which brought her to the bustling United Arab Emirates.

Self-described as lonely girl and blondeambition007 on internet blog sites; she decided to write an autobiography on her trials, tribulations and amazing life experiences. Growing up in the US opened Jayme's eyes to first hand stereo-typing and misconceptions of other cultures and places around the world.

Through travel and meeting people, she has seen the truth and beauty of life that she hopes to capture and highlight in this book.

www.daredreamdiscover.com

JAYME HARRIS

DARE, DREAM, DISCOVER

AS TOLD TO

TRUDY MARSHALL-BOWLER

EMERALD
BOOK CO.

Published by Emerald Book Company
4425 Mo Pac South, Suite 600
Longhorn Building, 3rd Floor
Austin, TX 78735

Distributed by Emerald Book Company

For ordering information or special discounts for bulk purchases, please contact Emerald Book Company at 4425 Mo Pac South, Suite 600, Longhorn Building, 3rd Floor, Austin, TX 78735, (512) 891-6100.

Cover design by Greenleaf Book Group LLC

ISBN: 978-1-934572-01-6

Printed in the United States of America on acid-free paper

08 09 10 11 12 13 14   10 9 8 7 6 5 4 3 2 1

First Edition

www.daredreamdiscover.com

CONTENTS

FOREWORD

WHEN I FIRST MET JAYME, I WAS STILL RECOVERING FROM MY HUSBAND'S TOUR IN IRAQ. We had been struggling pretty hard due to the fact that my husband had come home to discover, thanks to the poor economy in Michigan, that he would be out of work for six months. His employer wanted him to come back to work, but first they had to have work to offer anyone. The economy in Michigan was only getting worse and work was becoming tough to find in any field.

I was becoming increasingly frustrated by the fact that my last writing job had been a column in the newspaper near my husband's National Guard unit's home base and I was desperate for something that would make it look like we would have a hope for a better life at some point. I have written since my early teens and I really wanted to write for a living but, without a college degree, I had limited opportunities to find a job.

I ran across Jayme's blog one day and the title struck me. "Lonely Girl." I had spent most of my life feeling lonely and I wondered if this person would have any idea what it really felt like to be lonely. As I began to read her various blog entries, I realized this woman knew a great deal about being lonely, and somehow I felt as if this was a person who really understood what was really important in life. My heart broke for her as she talked about her mother and the man that she loved so much but didn't return her love in the same way.

In many ways I felt like I had found a soul mate. We lived very different lives; I was a housewife in a small town in Michigan that didn't even offer cable TV and she was living large in a place that sounded amazing to me. She had all of the things I had only dreamed of having, but I had the one thing in this world that she would have given it all up for: a family.

One day, I don't even recall how we found ourselves on the subject, Jayme suggested I write a blog about my greatest wish. I had two wishes. The first was to write for a living, and the second was to take my husband to the ocean without Iraq hanging over our heads. You see, my husband and I visited the ocean in New Jersey in December of 2004, a few days before he headed for Iraq. He had never seen the ocean before, and that day got me through the year with him being in Iraq. I was determined to bring him home safe and sound and go back to the ocean when we could just enjoy the day without knowing that we would have to say goodbye in a few days, without wondering if he would ever set foot on American soil, let alone the ocean beach again.

I wrote the blog and put it all out there and the next thing I know there was an e-mail from Jayme asking me to help her write her book. To be honest, I thought she was either crazy or full of it at that point. But, she had given me no reason to believe either in the past, so I decided to take the chance and see what happened. Within less than two weeks, I had a signed contract in my hand and I spent many moments just standing in the middle of my front yard or my living room and letting out a squeal of pure joy. I decided when the book was finished, my husband and I would go to the ocean. Once again, Jayme had other ideas; she decided I needed to go to Florida and see where she came from. Labor Day weekend of 2006, my husband and I once again stood on an ocean beach with nothing on our minds but the beauty of that ocean. My two biggest wishes in life had come true.

One of Jayme's favorite charities is called The Dream

DARE, DREAM, DISCOVER

Project. That has always seemed so fitting to me because Jayme is a person who not only believes in dreams, she makes them come true as well.

I find that I spend a good deal of time telling Jayme to get some rest, as it seems she is always working, and when work is going well, she seems happy. The happiest I have ever heard her sound was after she came back from Iraq and went back to working with government contracting. But even as happy as that makes her, I still hear a tone of sadness in her voice. Jayme wants the love and the family that most of us want, and I can't wait to see her have that in her life. Nobody with a heart like Jayme's can possibly be denied the love she so deserves.

On a more personal level: Jayme is not just my employer, nor is she just a book to me; she is someone who has been there as a friend during a serious crisis in my own life, and she has good humor and a great heart. When I close the last page of this book, I won't be closing it on Jayme. I suspect she will always be someone that I am proud to call friend. Jayme gave me the courage to dream and the tools to fulfill not just this dream but all of my dreams.

– Trudy Marshall-Bowler

INTRODUCTION

DARE, DREAM, DISCOVER IS BASED ON MY LIFE EXPERIENCES FROM THE US AIR FORCE TO THE MIDDLE EAST AND BEYOND.......

I don't like it when people use the "Victim Mentality" excuse; I can swap stories with the best of them. Dysfunction junction is where I grew up, but I'm glad because every experience has brought me to the place I am today. I get lonely, sad, and depressed from time to time, but that is fine with me because those are human emotions and I experience them. I don't think people should suppress sadness and bad memories; instead, learn from things that have happened to you and make something positive out of it. I have done a lot of positive things and have been part of a lot of great things in my lifetime. If I had played the victim all of my life, I would have never been able to move on and be an encouragement for other people's lives.

It is my greatest wish to give hope to troubled teens and people who have had all the odds against them growing up. It is important to keep our dreams alive and reach for the stars. It is important to keep our childlike thinking. When we are young we actually believe anything is possible, but as we grow older we have people who try to steal our dreams and tell us that we have to live a certain way or settle for less than what we want or deserve.

It is so easy to get caught up in how society tells us to think and act. We become brainwashed into stereotyping and unknowingly discriminating against other people, cultures, and different locations of the world. I have been so blessed to meet some of the most wonderful people of this earth. If I had listened to the general mindset of most of the people that surrounded me growing up–including the media, church, family, friends and co-workers–I would never have left the US to live my great adventures of traveling and really experiencing life.

Nothing great comes without taking risks. My favorite saying is something my father once told me: "The easiest road traveled is not necessarily the best or wisest choice." It can hurt to grow and learn, but by doing this you are forced to challenge certain things that you have grown up believing all of your life. Living in your comfort zone will not take you to new heights. Living in your

INTRODUCTION

comfort zone will get you the same results day after day. If you are happy with that, great, if not, stop griping and complaining about your life and the world we live in and make a difference in your life and others'. Seriously, don't we have enough negativity around us? Don't feed into negativity. It is a choice to be positive and contribute to life, society, and this world in a positive way.

You do not have to travel around the world like I have done; start with your own family and community. We cannot afford to waste time and energy focusing on the negative and everything that is wrong in life.

There are people in our families, communities, country, and world that are depending on us to help them. Just think, there is some little girl or boy, or someone in a nursing home waiting for you right now.

Focus on doing positive things and helping other people. You will be surprised at how much joy, happiness, and prosperity that will bring. Thank God for the person who first believed in me and told me so at the age of 18. She made a difference in my life, and it caused a huge and beautiful ripple effect that has allowed me to help family and friends be successful and happier in life. I have been able to provide a home for a family overseas that crossed my path in life that lost their home in the war in the Balkans. I have created hundreds of jobs for unemployed people of various nationalities and religious backgrounds around the world. After serving 11 years at Eglin Air Force Base, I have proudly supported our US troops in Kosovo, Iraq, Kuwait, and Pakistan. I continue to fly into Iraq and other war-torn locations and for relief aid after devastating acts of nature such as the earthquake in Pakistan. I also am the Managing Partner for a real estate company in Dubai.

So, put your seatbelt on and get ready to take a journey around this world with me. I hope that I can convey my unique life experiences in a way that will open your mind to accepting and experiencing greater things in your life. I started out with big dreams as a little girl. I'm 34 now and feel that I have already experienced what most would think is a full life. There is still so much out there. I never want to stop learning and meeting new people. If you are not growing you are dying.

We are all connected in one way or another in this life with one another and that is the beauty of what I have learned so far. We are all humans, one species; why shouldn't we help each other more? Spreading more love, money, food, and assistance around this world can't be a bad thing, right?

There is never a better time than NOW to start making a difference in this world. I hope you enjoy reading about my experiences, hopes, and joys. Keep your dreams alive and help other people reach their dreams. You will live a rich and meaningful life if you practice this; it has worked for me. I wish you much success and happiness on your journey.

CHAPTER I

LONELY GIRL

It's funny how life works out. When I was a little girl in Plant City, Florida, I dreamed of being a famous movie star. I wanted to be among the beautiful people and the beautiful things that came with them. I wanted to be like them. I would imagine being surrounded by my own entourage as people clamored for my attention. I wanted to be glamorous. I remember a photo taken from my childhood at Disney World. I was four years old and even then I wanted to be glamorous. In the photo I have on a pair of really big sunglasses and on the back my mother wrote: "Jayme posing as a movie star."

As I got older my idea of glamour changed with the times. I remember begging my mother to buy me sexy nightgowns when I was eight. My step-father was dead set against the idea of an eight year old running around in sexy anything. He made it adamantly clear that I was way too young to be wearing anything of the sort. Of course at eight I didn't understand the implications of sexy clothing,

LONELY GIRL

I just wanted to feel glamorous, like my favorite TV characters. I loved watching Nicolette Sheridan, as Paige on Knot's Landing, grace my TV screen in her beautiful clothes with a confident air. She had men fighting to be with her; a mother who, although a bit dysfunctional, still loved her very much; and an adoring father. I also got the sense that Paige wasn't entirely happy.

Maybe I liked her character so much because I was able to identify with the emptiness in her heart that seemed to resonate from the screen. She had the glamour and the excitement, but she didn't have what she was looking for: true love and acceptance.

Morgan Fairchild was another favorite of mine. As Richard Channing's attorney Jordan on Falcon Crest, she was a force to be reckoned with. This was a formidable woman who would not be bullied or backed down. She fought for the things that mattered to her and even the cruel and intimidating Angela Channing could not back the beautiful Jordan into a corner.

I guess I was taken by the bigger-than-life blonde women. Maybe it was because I was blonde, but as I look back I think it is because I saw something in them that touched my heart. Nicolette's character Paige was a reminder of the emptiness and loneliness in my own life. While her father loved her dearly and would do anything in the world for her, he had not been there for much of her life. For that reason I think she felt a bit rejected and left her searching for something to replace what was missing in her life. She was lonely, she was hurting; so was I.

Morgan's character Jordan was different. She was strong, determined, and in control of her own life. I wanted that so desperately for my own life. I didn't want others making decisions for me; I wanted to make my own. My life was out of control due to the adults around me; I would have given anything to have some of the control that Jordan exhibited. I never dreamed that one day my life would often mirror much of these two characters.

After much begging and pleading I did actually get the sexy nightgown and robes. They were so beautiful. I remember feeling like I was floating around the house in them. I would spend hours spinning and dancing around like I was already a glamorous movie star. They made me feel beautiful and special. I dreamed that I would find my Prince Charming while wearing something equally as beautiful when I grew up.

I had a prince, but he was far away in another state. I missed my dad terribly and I missed feeling wanted and loved. With my dad I always felt like a princess. I felt like I was the most important person in his world and I knew he loved me. I lived every day of the year waiting for summer and winter breaks so I could be with him; this was the only time I didn't feel like an outsider looking in. When I was with my dad, I felt like I belonged, but the rest of the time I felt alone, more alone than anyone, more than a child should ever feel. I would spend hours looking at the photograph from my dad's wedding to my step-mother. There with them I was part of a family, I wasn't alone.

Of course I always knew that was only a temporary reprieve from the isolated and empty life that I lived in the real world. During the rest of the year I would hold tight to that photo and that memory of a happy, loving family, and it would get me through another day.

I don't know if my mother knew how truly unhappy I really was. I don't know if she would have cared if she did know. All I know is that I was sad, alone, and often afraid of what would happen next.

DARE, DREAM, DISCOVER

There was a point when I could have spent all the time in the world with my dad. I didn't take advantage of that and now I live with the knowledge that it's too late to get the time back. I wonder if I would have done anything differently had I known what would have happened.

Would I have taken the time? Would I have said all the things that now run through my head when I think of him? Would my life be different had I done things in another way with my dad? I guess I will never know the answer to those questions, and knowing that I will never find out what often haunts my soul. Sometimes when I am alone late at night, I think about all of the "should haves" and "could haves." I never imagined that my dad wouldn't always be here, but it didn't work out that way. My dad lost a battle with cancer, and I lost the chance to spend more time with him.

It's easy for me to become that child again. I still spend too much time alone and I still dream of having a prince ride in on a white horse and rescue me from the emptiness of the world that I often live in.

Outwardly, I appear to have everything: money, jewelry, a nice car, a wonderful home, and I am surrounded by the beautiful people of the world. I fit in well and I am successful, but at the end of the day I go home and order take-out or stick something in the microwave and curl up with my television set or my laptop.

There is nobody to cuddle up to and make fun of the stupid television shows with me, there isn't someone to tell me that I am working too hard, there isn't someone to reach out in the middle of the night to pull me close, and there isn't someone to wipe away the tears when I feel like I am the loneliest woman in the world. My adult life, much like my childhood, has only me to take care of myself.

While many might ask me why on earth I feel like my life is still empty when I have all of these wonderful things, I expect they have never really been alone. Expensive clothes and jewelry will never make anyone totally happy. They might mask the sad exterior and make it look prettier, but they will never fill a sad and lonely heart.

CHAPTER II

THINGS THAT MATTER

THIRTY YEARS AFTER MY TRIP TO DISNEY WORLD, I HAVE THAT LIFE OF GLAMOUR. I live in a private resort community, and my closets are filled with beautiful clothing and shoes. Who would have dreamed that the girl from Plant City, Florida who had to borrow clothes in order to have something that wasn't several sizes too small would be living large in a place that attracts the likes of Donald Trump and super model Naomi Campbell. Who would have imagined the journey called my life would bring me to a place in the Middle East that resembles a cross between Las Vegas and Disney World?

Sometimes when I sit and look around at my life, I think about my dreams of being a movie star and living the glamorous life. I remember when "Grease" made its debut on the big screen. I begged my mother to take me to see it, but my step-father felt it was inappropriate for someone my age.

I suppose my nagging and pleading finally got to my

mother because she did give in and, along with my step-father, we went to a local drive-in to see the movie. I was hooked. I quickly learned every word to every song of the soundtrack, and I couldn't stand in front of the mirror without my very own pair of glittery spandex pants that Olivia Newton-John wore in the final scenes.

As I stood in front of the mirror and sang my heart out trying to imitate the moves and facial expressions that I had seen on the big screen, I knew without a doubt that someday it would be more than a fantasy; I would make it happen. I would live a movie star's life and I would be the most glamorous woman at all of the fancy parties.

I've lived that life and I have been to those parties. I am surrounded by the richest of the rich and the most beautiful of the beautiful people and I have been inside their world. While some have had some true happiness, it seems for most they do what they have to do to maintain the status quo; they smile for the cameras and cry in the dark. The life of glamour has lost its shine for me in many ways.

By no means do I mean to imply that I don't have a good life, because I am grateful for everything I have, all that I have been through, and the fact that I am able to determine my own destiny in this world. But at the end of the day, one does have to wonder what life holds for a 34-year-old woman who is often told by total strangers how beautiful she is.

Yet, I spend my nights alone. I eat my meals alone, watch TV alone, and go to bed alone.

As my friends back home are meeting for dinner and a movie or getting together for birthday, holidays, and all the other events that gather people together, I am alone in my beautiful home with clothes and nice things but few friends. Is this the life I am meant to have? Can I find the things that my heart really desires? How does a girl from Florida find herself half-way across the world in Dubai living the good life and still feel like she's the loneliest girl in the world?

But I don't believe in feeling sorry for myself. I find it a waste of time and energy. Like most people in this world, I have never had anything simply handed to me. I did not always have it easy; life was often difficult for me while growing up. Yet, somehow I always managed to get through and come out better for each experience.

THINGS THAT MATTER

I spent a great deal of time growing up seeking love. Looking back, I realize that the things that have made me feel loved in life are the people that have reached out to help me the most.

During high school, my best friend Alison and her family took me in when my mother abandoned me. The firefighters I worked with were the closest thing I had at the time to brothers and father figures; they didn't cut me any slack, but that made me strong and I grew so much from that.

There were people in the fire department that were against me simply because I was a woman, but there were also people that believed in me and encouraged me every step of the way.

There are pros and cons to everything I have been through in life. I accept and appreciate everything that I have been through and every person in my life because they have made me the person that I am today and have brought me to where I am today.

I still have a lot to learn and I look forward to the challenges. I still get e-mails from Blerta, a girl whose family I helped in Kosovo, telling me how much they love their new home and that they want me to come and visit. I am happy that I was able to help someone get a home and make their life a little better. I know what that feeling is like because Alison's mother took me in and made my life better, so it is nice to pass that on to as many people as I can.

I still love this adventure I call my life. I love the excitement and glamour, but today it is in perspective and I know that there is more to life than fancy clothes and cars. I want more than the material and the recognition; I want real love and a real family, but sometimes I wonder if it's out of my reach or if I have to compromise my love for adventure in order to have those things.

CHAPTER III

MY PARENTS

ON MARCH 12, 1972, I WOULD MAKE MY FIRST APPEARANCE INTO THIS WORLD IN MIAMI, FLORIDA. I was the first child of Jim and Cindy Harris. My father had been in the Air Force and served in Vietnam before he met my mother. My mother was a 17-year-old cheerleader at a Miami high school, and I am told it was love at first sight for both of my parents one night after a football game. It was a whirlwind romance; my mother dropped out of high school and they married a few days before her 18th birthday.

Even though it was love at first sight, it became obvious that looks can be deceiving; the marriage ended just four years later. My mother and I moved from place to place over the next several months. I remember living in a trailer at one time, and after that we moved in with my grandparents. It wasn't long before my mother met a new man and began dating him. Sometime around my fourth birthday my mother introduced me to a man named Randy.

MY PARENTS

Randy owned a concrete company and it appeared that he did well for himself. Soon I would find myself living in a nice house with Randy and my mother.

From the first time I met this man he made me uncomfortable. They say a child has good instincts and mine were telling me that I did not like this man. First he tried buying me off. He would bring me presents and treats and for each he insisted he should get a kiss or a hug for his bribes. I hated this man and I did not want him touching me let alone having to give him physical affection. When that didn't work he turned mean. I remember there were times when he would be eating something and I would ask for some. Instead of letting me have any, he would simply get up and throw away whatever was left. I finally gave up asking for anything from him as I knew there was no way he would give it to me.

Much to my chagrin he did not go away. My mother seemed intent on making this man my new daddy, and she married him within six months of meeting him.

My mother was a beautiful woman. Though she wasn't model tall, she was about 5'5" with long toned legs that were almost always tanned. She often highlighted her dark hair with blonde streaks so it looked like it had been lightened naturally by the sun. She was very aware of her appearance and was not afraid to use her beauty to get what she wanted.

My mother never did anything half way. When my mother decided to sell Tupperware, she put her all into it and very quickly moved up and earned her way to being a top seller. Like everything my mother did, when she put her mind to it she did better than most. Simply by selling plastic bowls, as many now describe the business, my mother made a good deal of money and actually did well enough that she drove around in a station wagon provided by Tupperware. She seemed to be the Tupperware Queen of Plant City, Florida, and she thrived on her success.

For those who knew her, my mother's looks were not what made her different from all of the other moms around town. My mother had a history of erratic and unpredictable behavior and often it was scary. Though never diagnosed with any particular mental illness, I have my own suspicions. As much effort as she put into selling Tupperware, she would put the same effort into other things as well. My mother never stuck to any one thing for too long; she would go from being the most devout Christian–reading, quoting, and demanding we all live by the bible–to dressing and behaving like some kind of sex kitten. My best friend Alison remembers different phases of my mother's religious journeys: "One week she would be going to church every single day and everything was about her church and beliefs, and then the next week it might be Halloween and she would be dressed as if she were in one of those adult-type cartoons." I expect her behavior and dramatic personality changes shocked Alison and my other friends, but for me this was simply the way my mother was and I was used to it.

My step-father Randy genuinely did not like me. I would venture to go as far as to say he hated me. He hated it when my mother would give me any kind of attention, and he made it clear that he would make my life hell for being in the way. Looking back as an adult, I have to wonder what actually caused his feelings toward me.

Was I in the way? Was I a reminder that my mother had been with and loved someone else before him? Had it been my own behavior when he came into my mother's life that made him dislike me or was I simply acting on gut instinct? Would he have treated me differently had I been nicer to him then? Of course, in all reality, I was the child and he was the adult, therefore he should have known better, but trying to determine what might have made things different will not change the past so I don't spend much time dwelling on it.

Randy was the primary parent in our home. Although my mother was there, Randy laid down the rules and enforced the discipline. I remember being hit with a belt often, but what I didn't know was this would not be the worst of what he did to me at least the physical punishment didn't put me on display for the rest of the world to see my pain, but that would change.

I refused to call him dad, and while it seemed to be a source of contention between us, I held my ground. He wasn't my dad; I had a dad and I missed him greatly. This seemed to work until I turned six.

My mother became pregnant and gave birth to a baby girl. Randy had decided that, since the baby would be named Randi, I must start calling him dad because it would be too confusing for the baby. By this point I had learned to do as I was told if I wanted to avoid his wrath. It seemed as if the impending arrival of his own child only made him hate me even more, and now he decided I would start cleaning the house.

I remember him putting me up on a stool to do the dishes and drawing a picture on a piece of paper to show me in exactly what order the dishes were to be washed. I had to start with the silverware first, then glasses and cups, then plates, and finish with pots and pans. Any deviation from his precise drawing would make him angry and I would be punished in some way. I didn't like being spanked, so I always tried to do exactly as the chart showed.

I came to hate eating, and dinner was the worst for me. I conjured up an imaginary dog in my head and I would throw my food under the table to the dog. In my child's mind I honestly believed that there really was a dog and I really believed that he would eat my food. I decided that the food really wasn't very good, especially meatloaf (I hated meatloaf), because even the dog didn't eat it.

This seemed like a great plan until I got caught. I was required to always clean my plate no matter how much food was on it or how much I hated what I was being fed.

DARE, DREAM, DISCOVER

When Randy and my mother found the meatloaf under the table, I was forced to eat an entire pan of the awful stuff. Many times I would end up being made to eat so much that I would become physically ill.

While I don't like to consider myself as someone who was abused, I suspect many might see it as such. For me this was simply my way of life and I did what I had to in order to get through each and every day.

Upon the arrival of my sister, my mother went into a deep depression. From that point on, I don't remember ever getting much attention from her unless it was negative. My mother had wanted a boy, but instead she had another daughter and she was anything but pleased about this.

Instead of taking care of her child, I was left babysitting my infant sister at the age of six. Randy would be at work and my mother had taken on a job at a local convenience store. I remember often being scared and calling her at work. She would yell at me for bothering her at work and that would be the end of that. It didn't matter that I was afraid, it didn't matter that I was way too young to take care of myself, let alone an infant. I learned at a very young age to change diapers, mix formula, feed a baby, and all the other things that a new mother would usually do. I sometimes wonder how neither I nor my sister did not suffer some kind of serious injury during this time. Of course these days people know more about things such as post-partum depression and mental illness, but at that time a new mother was supposed to be thrilled with her new baby.

If anyone actually noticed something was wrong in our home, they never did or said anything to stop any of it. I don't know if my mother was suffering from post-partum or if it was the same instability that she has always suffered from all of my life, but it took its toll on my six-year-old psyche.

Things became even worse when my sister started walking. My mother was working the midnight shift and I had to take care of my sister while she worked or slept. One night I was left to babysit my sister and I fell asleep. My sister had gotten into my mother's make-up and colored the walls with her findings. When my mother and step-father came home, I was in big trouble. I woke up to my step-father screaming at me. I didn't know exactly what had happened, but it quickly became clear as I saw my sister's masterpiece all over the walls. It was the middle of the night and I had to get up and clean everything before I was put on restriction and spanked for falling asleep.

One day (I don't recall exactly what happened or why I was so scared) I called my mother at work and told her I wanted to go live with my dad. This obviously angered her as she said "FINE! I will disown you and nobody will ever know that I ever had a daughter."

Of course in my six-year-old mind there was no way she could simply pretend that I didn't exist, and I quickly informed her "They will know because they can look around and see all the pictures of me. People will ask about me and where I am."

I wasn't prepared for what she would come back with. "Well, we will just burn all of those pictures." It started to dawn on me that she would do it. She would make it appear as if I really had never been there. I couldn't believe that my own mother would simply make me disappear from her life and not care.

I desperately wanted to live with my dad, but things did not work out that way then. Of course, in my child's mind it should have, but at six years old who understands about things such as custody, work, childcare, and other things that only an adult should have to consider.

I always loved the phone calls from my dad as we would exchange words of our undying love for one another. He would tell me "I love you as big as the moon." I would then respond with "I love you as big as the sky." Of course, not letting me outdo him, he would reply "I love you as big as the universe."

We would continue with this for a long time; each time we would try to top the other with our love.

I felt entirely loved by my father and I worshipped him. However, all too often that worship was from afar. I still remember my first visit to my father when I was four years old. I felt so grown up flying on an airplane all by myself. When the plane landed and we arrived at the airport in Ohio, the flight attendant walked me off of the plane in her arms and asked me "Ok, where is your daddy? Pick him out." I found him and was so excited to see him. As the flight attendant handed me over I felt like a princess being handed over to her waiting prince. The only thing missing was his big white stallion to whisk me away with him, never having to return to my mother and her mood swings or my evil step-father.

When I would visit with my dad we would stay with his adopted mother. I loved staying with my grandma. She ran a small business in the front of her home, a ceramic shop. I loved this shop because I was able to sit there with all the other ladies and help paint the items. I loved the process of taking something as simple as a shaped piece of clay and turning it into something beautiful. I felt like I was helping and my grandma seemed to be pleased with that help. I had a feeling of accomplishment.

I'll never forget the day a wonderful, sweet lady walked into the shop. She had come to paint and I was immediately taken with her. She looked just like Snow White with beautiful eyes and fair skin; she even had her dark hair styled in that upturned bob like Snow White. Something about her felt peaceful and it drew me to her immediately. I liked the feeling of serenity when I was around her.

My mother was not a very loving or nurturing person, but this lady was kind and gentle. I remember as a child having imaginary visions of birds flying all around her just like the scene in Snow White. I knew they would simply fly to her and eat out of her hand if they were given the chance.

Her name was Sue, and as she sat there with me in the ceramic shop and taught me to paint, I fell in love with her. She spent time with me, she talked with me, she was kind to me, and she made me feel important. I hadn't had much of that from the adults around me back home and from my mother, but here in this ceramic shop I had all the love and attention I could soak in. I loved Sue's peaceful and nurturing ways, and I spent hours with her as she taught me to paint. I decided that day that this was the perfect woman for my dad.

As soon as my dad came home from work that night, I ran out to meet him. "Daddy, look who I met today!" I was excited as I pointed out my Snow White. Who better for Snow White than my own prince?

The next thing I knew, I was going out on a date with them. We went to the park and played on the swings together. I had so much fun with the two of them, I never wanted the day to end. Everything happened so fast with them, but soon they were getting married and I was the flower girl in their wedding.

When the summer ended I did not want to leave. I wanted to stay with my dad and my new step-mother. I was happy with them and I felt wanted when I was around them. But, again, I had to return to my mother's home with just the memory and a photograph of our happy family.

I don't know exactly what transpired between my parents during these years, but I remember they seemed to be constantly fighting about child support. In the end they went to court, and when all was said and done I don't believe that my dad had to pay support any longer.

My father always had a problem with my mother spending the child support on whatever suited her fancy instead of using it to take care of me.

My mother didn't seem to want me, and now she wasn't getting any money for me either. Sometime around the time I was in the third grade, my parents agreed to let me live with my dad. Although there had not been a change in custody, it was kind of a "let's see what happens" arrangement.

MY PARENTS

While I lived with my dad I had chores and he expected me to earn anything that I got, but I was treated well. However, I wasn't happy. My dad and step-mother were trying to start their own family, and even though they were never mean or cruel to me, I began to feel that I did not fit in. Also, all of my friends were in Florida.

In the end, I went back to my mother's home and never asked to move in with my dad again, but I never stopped missing him either.

CHAPTER IV

DYSFUNCTION JUNCTION

As THE YEARS PASSED, THINGS NEVER GOT MUCH BETTER, BUT MY MOTHER DID ADD A NEW TWIST TO THINGS. Sometime in my teens she started cheating on my step-dad. For my mother to cover her tracks, she had to make everything look innocent. She would say she was taking me someplace for school and then take me to meet her boyfriend.

I actually liked going with her, since she would often let me take a friend of mine. My friend and I could swim and have fun while my mother met her boyfriend. My mother would give us alcohol to bribe us. While I didn't really care for alcohol at that point in my life, my friend did. My mother didn't seem to be bothered by giving underage kids alcohol, and I wasn't going to complain because I was always hoping that the next man would be her new Mr. Right and she would leave my step-father.

I suppose this was when I started to realize that my mother had a way with men. She could get them to do just about anything she wanted them to do, and even when she treated them poorly they would come back begging for more. My mother was beautiful and she knew it. My mom would lay in the sun to tan and always had a strenuous work out routine, but in general she was blessed with both beauty and a naturally fit body and she enjoyed using them to get attention.

I remember my mom posing for a photo on top of the new Corvette my step-father had bought for her. She looked like one of those pin-up girls. Smiling and sexy, nobody would have ever dreamed of the monster that hid beneath the beautiful exterior. To me she was the devil in disguise. Showing her charm and beauty to draw in her prey and then spewing her evil upon anyone that got too close or cared about her.

I remember one time we went to a family water park in Florida. My mother had recently had breast enhancement surgery and was more than proud to show off her new trophies. The park had a bikini contest and my mother won. Given that my mother loved having her ego stroked, she ran with this. She wanted to enter more and take this further. At one point she even had her hair braided to look like Bo Derek.

DARE, DREAM, DISCOVER

This phase lasted for a short time, and my mother won a few more contests. Then she found religion again. She decided that having someone from the church see her on a billboard in a bikini or in seductive clothing would not reflect well on the new image she was trying to put forth. Of course, this was about as hypocritical as anyone could be in my mind. My mother never lasted very long as the good wife and mother, and I knew soon she would be off cheating again.

Her religious phases were the worst times for me because she expected perfection. I could barely breathe without her finding something wrong or sinful in my behavior. Even if I had been the perfect child and behaved exactly as she wanted, I believe she would have found fault with something.

I seemed to be her favorite target. I came to believe that my mother hated me and she did all she could to hurt me. Unless I was covering for her affairs or taking care of my sister or the house, she had no use for me. She claimed I had ruined her life and blamed me for all the bad things that happened in her life.

My mother's affairs would go on for the rest of

my childhood. She took to leaving for days with her boyfriends, making up these elaborate stories about going away with her girlfriends. She never seemed to feel any guilt or remorse about her affairs, and I hated my step-father so much that I always encouraged her to find more boyfriends. I didn't care who she was with, I just wanted to get away from the sadistic man that went out of his way to make my life hell. I was sure Randy knew about the affairs.

We lived in a small town and people were starting to talk, but he never said or did anything about any of it. He loved my mother and was he was afraid that she would leave him.

One of my mother's affairs sticks out in my mind more than the others. It happened when I was in the seventh grade. This relationship took a turn that the others had not; she became very serious about this particular man and she decided that she was going to leave my step-father. One night she sat down at the dinner table and informed Randy that she was leaving him. At the time I was on the phone with my boyfriend from school and didn't pay a whole lot of attention to the argument that ensued between the two of them.

DARE, DREAM, DISCOVER

My mother got up from the table and went over to the sink. I was sitting on the floor not too far from where she was standing when my step-father stood up and knocked my mother to the ground. He began to drag my mother across the house by her hair. Still holding onto her hair, he threw her out through the front door and onto the concrete sidewalk.

I screamed into the phone to my boyfriend, "Call 9-1-1! Call 9-1-1!" I hung up the phone, and then I realized Randy was now coming toward me. I took off running for the sliding glass door. While the main door opened, the screen door jammed. I was positive I was going to be his next target until, moments before he got to me, the door came loose and opened. I ran out of the house and around to the front screaming at the top of my lungs. I didn't see my mother and I wondered how she was, but I was determined to get away and get some kind of help.

We lived in a very isolated wooded area and I began to realize just how long that dirt road was as I ran in the direction of the nearest house screaming "Call 9-1-1!" as loud as I could. Unfortunately, there was nobody to hear or help me that night. To make matters worse, my boyfriend had not called 911 or anyone else, and even if he had it is doubtful that it would have done any good. We lived in the middle of nowhere and at that time most rural areas did not have 911 services. When I finally did reach another house, I was able to reach one of my mother's friends on the telephone to come and get us.

I remember when we returned to our house. I told my mother that we needed to get all of our clothes. My mother tried to calm me and told me "We will only be gone a few nights. Just get what you need for a couple of days; we can't take everything with us." But I kept insisting that we take everything. In the end I could not convince her to take more than enough for a few days, and she didn't bring anything that mattered to us. When we left we hadn't even gotten any of my own clothes and I left with nothing more than the clothes on my back.

The next night my mother called my step-father to tell him that she was coming with the police to get some things. I am not sure why she felt the need to warn him in advance. Maybe she thought that if he knew the police were coming as well that he would be on his best behavior. If that is what she was thinking, she could not have been more wrong, as she would soon discover.

When my mother arrived at the house with the police, they saw a huge bonfire in the front yard. Not sure what to think about the fire, my mother and the police went to the front door and knocked. Randy answered the door with a rather frightening smile on his face.

"Yes, can I help you?" he asked the police.

The police informed him that my mother was there to get her belongings. With a rather pleased look on his face, my step-father pointed to the fire and said "Help yourself."

He had not left one piece of clothing unburned that belonged to my mother or me. My sister had gone with us as well, and he left her stuff alone; I suppose he had some feelings for her as she was his child, but he did not show a scrap of compassion for either my mother or me.

Domestic violence was still one of those things that the police did not bother to get involved in during those days. If there was too much noise they would come and tell everyone to quiet down, but that was really all they did about such calls. My mother had not been seriously injured or even cut from her fall to the sidewalk, and now we were out of the house, so as far as the police were concerned they had done their job.

My mother tried another time to go back and get some furniture and other belongings. Again this did not fare well for her. This time my mother found herself with a gun held to her head, and in the end she decided that we didn't need anything out of that house any longer. The police were called, but they did nothing. It seemed Randy always got away with whatever he did.

My mother, sister, and I would live the remainder of the school year in the worst trailer I had ever seen in my life. Looking back, I wonder how this dilapidated piece of tin had not been condemned by the city; it seemed to be falling down around our ears. At night we would go to sleep with a pile of shoes next to the bed to chase away the rats we could hear eating away at our belongings, the walls, and whatever else might be in the closets. We would throw a shoe at the closet and the rats would quit for awhile, but we always knew they would be back as soon as things got quiet again. We didn't get much sleep. We would sleep for a bit, hear the gnawing, toss a shoe, and go back to sleep many times during the night.

DARE, DREAM, DISCOVER

We had gone from living in a nice and comfortable house in the country to living in a dump and having little money to survive. I am not sure why, but it seemed the only thing we ate that year was corned beef and cabbage. On a rare occasion my mother would make a cheesecake as a treat, but dinner every night was corned beef and cabbage. While I hated my step-father and did not want to go back, this was not an easy adjustment for me. My mother was working two jobs to support us, and I don't think my dad was paying child support anymore, but from time to time I would intercept a $100.00 check from him. I believe he was trying to help us out when he could.

The following year I went into the eighth grade, and I never imagined how crazy our life would get during that time. My mother had started driving a bus for the school system. One of her routes took her near our old house. One afternoon as she was driving in the area she noticed a good deal of smoke nearby. She said she had thought to herself that it was awfully close to the old house but didn't really think much of it at the time.

My step-father was still living in the house; it was in his name and there was no way my mother could afford the payments. Later that afternoon my mother received a phone call telling her that the house had burned to the ground. Nothing was salvageable. Anything that had been left in the house when we moved out was gone. Photos, keepsakes, furniture, and everything else in the house had been destroyed. Again, our lives had gone up in smoke with nobody to help us recover any of it.

Soon after the smoke cleared, the investigation began, and it was discovered that the fire had not been an accident. Two juvenile boys from the neighborhood confessed to intentionally setting the fire and told the police that my step-father had hired them. They gave details right down to the accelerant they had used to set the fire and explained that my step-father had given them money to burn the house down.

During the time after we moved out, my mother and step-father reconciled and broke-up again several times. I never understood why they kept going back to one another; they were poison to each other and they kept taking in the toxins the other was feeding them. How does a woman go back and sleep with a man that held a gun to her head? I will never understand that. There was one time that my mother suspected Randy was seeing another woman, so we went to visit her house. It was sometime around Christmas and she had her tree up. I began looking at the decorations. There was one similar to one I had made when I was in elementary school. It was a bell made out of cardboard and tin foil. I even commented on the fact that I had made one. The more I looked at the tree, the more things I found that looked just like the ornaments that we had before we left Randy's house. Little by little it came together.

Randy had given her our decorations and now she had them hanging on her tree! Even the ornaments made by my sister and me. Why would anyone want the homemade things of another woman's children? I pointed out to my mother that many seemed to be ones that had come from our house. My mother kept trying to hush me but I was bothered by the fact that our things were in this woman's house. Why my mother just wanted to let it all go was shocking to me.

Looking back now, I realize that my step-father was taking things out of the house before the fire. But why was he taking things that really should not have held any value to him because they were made by me is something I will never entirely understand.

DYSFUNCTION JUNCTION

After the fire and the confession and the allegations of my step-father paying them to set the fire, there had been some problems with getting the insurance check. I am not sure exactly what happened or how things transpired, but by the time all was said and done my mother and my step-father were back together fighting the charges together. Somehow they did end up getting the insurance check and they began rebuilding their home.

We all ended up living with my step-father's family while the house was rebuilt. As much as he hated me, his mother hated me even more and never hesitated to make it very clear in her treatment of me. I could deal with her hate far easier than I could deal with living in her house. The house was filthy and infested with cockroaches.

One afternoon, I was hungry and decided to cook a hot dog. I went to check on the hot dog and there in the boiling water was a cockroach sitting on my hot dog. I decided I wasn't so hungry after all. I have never been so glad to move into a new house as I was that summer before ninth grade. Finally! A clean house without cockroaches or rats. I didn't care where we lived as long as it was free of bugs and filth.

DARE, DREAM, DISCOVER

Soon my mother was back in one of her religious phases again, so we were going to church twice on Sunday, Wednesday night, and doing all kinds of volunteer work as well. I was starting to enjoy this time. Even though I knew my mother was a hypocrite, I still like what I was getting from being around the church. I decided instead of worrying about who was giving the message that I would just take the message to heart. I found strength and solace in my new-found beliefs.

Of course, my mother's religious phase only lasted until she met a new boyfriend. She was working the late shift in a convenience store, so what could be more convenient for her than a late-duty police officer who would stop in for a coffee break every night?

Things became very, very strange at this point. Both were married and both had either a twisted sense of humor or simply felt they were untouchable because they had become quite gutsy in their relationship. He would bring his family to our home and my mother would make a nice dinner for all of us. I wondered if his wife and my step-father had any idea that they were being made fools of as we all sat and chatted through our nicely prepared meals. Maybe someone did realize that there was something going on at the time, as my mother and step-father started going to marriage counseling.

I had always had a great deal of responsibility around the house. My sister, who seemed to have checked out from life and almost never spoke, had no chores or responsibilities, while I was left to care not only for her but also the house. Imagine my surprise when my parents came home one night and explained that they were going to make some changes in our lives.

I didn't really know what to expect, but I know I was not anticipating four pages of yellow legal paper with new chores and responsibilities for me. My sister basically got a pat on the head and sent on her way; I on the other hand apparently was not living up to my end of the work in our household. I would now become responsible for sweeping the porch and sidewalk every day to clear the oak leaves. Even to this day, I consider oak leaves my enemy. I would also scrub the pool walls in the backyard for algae; there were times that I was positive that my arms would fall off. I was responsible for doing the laundry of everyone in the house, scrubbing all three bathrooms, and more. To make matters worse, I was only allotted five minutes a day of phone time and found myself missing out on a great deal of my teenage life.

This was also about the time that my step-father had found a new way to torture me when I made him angry: he would put me on restriction. His concept of restriction was to take away buying school clothes for me for that year. From about seventh grade on I never got school clothes again. I had to borrow clothes from my sister, who was six years younger, or from friends.

On occasion my mother and I would share clothing, but normally the clothes were cast-offs from my sister. I was rather small so it wasn't a big problem when it came to size, but with the six years between us there was a definite difference in style, and it was humiliating to realize I didn't have any clothes of my own.

The marriage counseling didn't seem to work very well for my mother and step-father. One morning I came home after being granted a rare overnight stay with a friend. When I came through the door, my step-father was waiting for me. He was standing there in the dark, visibly upset and angry.

"Do you know where your mom is?" he demanded of me. Of course I didn't know; I had been gone all night, and now I was wondering what in the heck was going on. "Nobody has seen her in over twenty four hours. She left her shift at work and she hasn't come home."

I stood there in the dark thinking that he must have killed her. I had always figured that Randy would lose his temper with her over one of her affairs and end up killing her, and now I was sure that was exactly what he had done. If he hadn't killed her, then I was sure she had run off with the cop and I was still worried Randy might kill me in my sleep.

Randy started yelling and screaming about my mother leaving him, leaving us, and what a whore she was. I didn't know what to do; what could I do? I was getting really scared because now I was left alone with a man that hated me.

For the next few days I went back and forth in my mind trying to decide which was actually the real truth, because both scenarios were very possible.

My questions were answered about a week later. My mother's car was found parked at a truck stop not too far away from home with a note on the windshield. It said that we were better off without her. I was furious with her. How could she just up and leave without so much as a good bye or anything? How could she put us all through the worry and the stress of not knowing what had happened to her. How could she leave her children behind? How could she leave me with a man that hated me? She missed my first prom.

I was in the ninth grade and I was so proud of the fact that I had been asked to go to the prom with a really cute guy from the eleventh grade. I was so proud and excited to be going, and now my mother would miss one of the biggest events of my young life and she didn't even care.

I decided I was glad she was gone; I didn't care if she ever came back. In fact, I hoped she wouldn't. I wouldn't have to live with her dual personalities of whore and ultra-religious bible thumper anymore. I wouldn't have to live with her insults, her mood swings, or her tantrums. I wouldn't have to wonder from one minute to the next what she was going to do or how she was going to hurt me. Things seemed to improve between me and my step-father during this time. He was nicer to me, and I took care of the house, the meals, my sister, and anything else that would come up during this time. Nobody said I had to do this, it just seemed to me like it was what I was supposed to do, so I went about it and did what needed to be done.

I didn't tell my dad what was going on because I was afraid he would be worried, and I didn't want to impose on his life with his new family. I had good friends who helped me out when I needed it. My best friend Alison and her parents were so good to me. Alison would let me borrow her clothes when I wanted, plus we worked with her dad to get extra cash, so I could actually buy some clothes for myself.

I loved working with Alison's dad. He was an electrician and he used to save all the extra wiring for us. We would collect all the scrap wire and take it out back to burn it down. Once we burned off all the coating, we were left with a big pile of copper. We had to wait overnight for it to cool because the kerosene would burn for hours, so the copper was incredibly hot. Once it cooled, we had to shake it all off and separate it all into large barrels. By the time we were done we were covered in black soot from head to toe. We would then load it up into the truck and take it in and sell it. We would often get over a few hundred dollars each. I had spending money, clothes, and sort of an extended family to me. I had a life, and I was beginning to find my own way.

I did not want my mother coming back, and I did not want her and Randy to get back together, so I set Randy up with one of my friend's moms during that time. They went out on a date, but nothing seemed to really come of it. We were beginning to feel something like a normal family and, while my life wasn't perfect, it wasn't so bad either. I might not have been the happiest teen in the world, but I was happy enough. Life wasn't always crazy and I wasn't walking on eggshells every minute of the day.

This was the only time I ever remember my step-father getting mad at my sister. One day, she must have really been missing our mother and, as young as she was, I don't think she really understood what had happened and that our mother had left without any intention of returning to us, my sister asked my step-father when mom was coming home. My sister didn't talk very often as it was, so I can only imagine what it was like to have her father react by screaming and yelling at her.

"Your mother is never coming back; she is nothing but

a whore!" he ranted and raved for sometime.

I found myself feeling sorry for my sister. She was young and scared, and this only made things worse for her. I sat and held her for quite some time after this; I wanted to comfort her, I wanted her to believe that everything would be alright. She had been like a zombie most of her childhood and now that she had actually spoken up and asked a question she found that she was met with rage and anger. It was no wonder the only thing she really seemed to do was sit in front of the television for hours upon hours. I expect she was shutting the rest of the world out.

A few months later my mother started calling. I refused to talk to her as she tried telling me that everything she was doing was for me. She reminded me that she had only married my step-father to take care of me and now she had run off with this man for me. She was going to make a lot of money and give me things that I had never had before. I didn't want to hear it. My mother was a master salesperson and I had no intentions of buying her latest wares. She had lied to me so many times in the past, she would make promises that only lasted as long as I did what she wanted and then they were forgotten. I was tired of empty promises, lies, and her. I simply did not want to hear anymore. I prayed she would stay wherever she was and never come back. I believed what she wrote on her note when she left: we were better off without her.

When trying to buy me off didn't work, my mother started calling and talking to my step-father. I tried to warn him. "She is playing you. She will just hurt you again. You know what she is like." I knew without a single doubt that she would cheat on him again and she would leave again. We were doing fine on our own and I knew if she came back she would turn our lives inside-out again. He insisted that he wasn't going to be taken in again by her; he promised me he wouldn't take her back, but I knew in my heart that in the end he would give in to her and give her whatever she wanted.

It started when Randy told me that my mother was coming home for a visit. He insisted that I go with him and my sister to the airport to pick her up. I was disgusted, and the look on my face when I saw her let her know just how I felt about the entire situation. I knew that was to be the beginning of the end, and I was right. It didn't take more than a couple of days before I realized they were getting back together and she was back to stay.

DYSFUNCTION JUNCTION

My mother likely felt betrayed by me because I wasn't thrilled to have her back home and I wouldn't buy into her lies when she called while she was gone. Now she was going to make sure I paid dearly for my betrayal. She decided that until I learned to be respectful, I would lose privileges. She took my phone away, I could not see any of my friends, and I couldn't go anywhere but to church with the family. I felt as if I was being blackmailed into having a relationship with her.

Of course the question was always which "her" was I having the relationship with? In public she was a loving and caring mother, while behind closed doors she was a manipulative and vindictive monster who wanted what she wanted and didn't care about the price others might have to pay for her actions. The woman genuinely hated me, and yet she wanted respect and love from me, I wanted no part of that.

I threatened to tell Randy what she was doing to me. I believed that Randy and I had built some kind of loyalty between us during the time my mother was gone. I figured that caring for him and my sister had to count for something with him, but my mother knew that she had the upper hand. She told me "You go right ahead and tell him whatever you want. He will do whatever I tell him to do because he loves me."

Of course my mother was right. Any loyalty that I thought might be there was non-existent. Randy was back to treating me the way he had always treated me before: humiliating me in any way he could.

Alison remembers one night when she had come to my house and we went out somewhere and left her Jeep behind. She had been given a Jeep 4x4 for her 16th birthday and we loved that Jeep, but for some reason we left the Jeep at my house that night only to return and find insanity ensuing.

Randy had called Alison's house and her mother answered. He started screaming into the phone that someone had better come and get the Jeep out of his yard before he had it towed away or something worse. Needless to say her parents were very upset and came to pick up the Jeep, but Randy had the Jeep towed before they even reached the house, which was less than 20 minutes away. Randy was still ranting and raving when we arrived. I was mortified. I wasn't surprised, but this particular outburst was not something I had anticipated or I would have never let Alison leave her Jeep there.

As a result, Alison's parents didn't want her hanging out with me because they feared for their daughter's safety. That was devastating for me because Alison and her family were basically the only physical and emotional support that I had. I still couldn't understand why Randy and my mother insisted on making my life a living hell.

To make matters worse, my mother seemed to be jealous of the relationship I had with the boy I was dating. She would tell me I wasn't good enough for him and that he didn't really care about me. When trying to destroy my confidence and self-esteem didn't work, she started hitting on him. It seemed to me that she was jealous of me and hated it when anyone cared about me or gave me any kind of positive attention. She would do whatever she could to take that attention away from me.

I was furious with my mother and my first instinct was to rebel. I quickly discovered this would get me no place with her, but it did get me on restriction for up to six months at one point. Slowly I learned to play the game and simply keep my mouth shut. I wanted my freedom, I needed to be out of the house, and the only way to do that was to treat her with respect. I did what I had to do to earn my freedom back. I may have treated her respectfully, but I never respected her, and as time went by I simply lived for the day I could leave her house for good and never look back. I was a survivor, I would survive, I had to survive, and I would show them all that I was not going to be broken.

Before I graduated from high school, my mother proved that what I told my step-father was true: it was not long at all until she was back to her old habit of cheating and leaving. They broke up and got back together several times before they finally divorced.

For the next couple of years I became accustomed to the fact that I might come home on any given day after school to find that my mother would be gone without explanation and without anyone to take care of even my most basic needs. On rare occasions she would also leave my sister behind, but more often than not she took my sister when she left. I was always the one she left behind.

CHAPTER V

NEW BEGINNINGS

DURING THE TIMES MY MOTHER WAS GONE, I LEARNED WHAT IT FELT LIKE TO BE HUNGRY. She didn't leave any food in the house. Sometimes there would be a bag of potatoes or some other small staple in the house. There were times that I would eat fried potatoes until they were gone, and then I scrounged for whatever I could find to eat. Many times I would find change and scrape that together to get a package of crackers and some juice at school. I made a habit of finding someplace off by myself to eat because I didn't want anyone else to know what was going on. I was embarrassed and scared.

Alison's mother knew that I was alone and often tried to get me to come eat with them, but I hated feeling indebted to anyone, so I would usually refuse. I was always invited to come spend holidays with them but usually I just stayed home, so she would bring me over a plate of food. My boyfriend also knew what was going on, and from time to time he would bring me pizza or something else to eat. Somehow I managed to survive every time my mother would abandon me, but each time she came back, I always knew there would be a next time.

We lived in an isolated area, and even when my mother was home she was gone a lot, so I don't think the neighbors were really aware that she had left me behind. I had learned to take care of myself, I had learned to take care of others, and I knew no matter what anyone did in the future, I would make it and I would survive.

Life pretty much went this way throughout my high school years, and then my mother dropped a bomb on me during my senior year. "We're moving to Cocoa Beach," she informed me one day. I was devastated. What did she mean we were moving? It was my senior year! I could not switch schools NOW; there was no way I would graduate. I was already struggling with school and now she wanted to move me half way across the state?

I talked with Alison and her parents, and her mother invited me to stay with them for the remainder of the school year. This would be perfect! I would not have to worry about food, I would not have to worry about clothes (since I could work for Alison's dad and make enough to have a decent wardrobe), I would not have to worry about the lights, the phone, or anything else being turned off, and I would not have to worry about my mother's mood swings or violent tantrums. At least for the last part of my childhood I could live a normal, peaceful life.

When I first met Alison, her mom couldn't believe some of the things I had told her about my mother. She thought I might be exaggerating to get attention or to make my mother seem worse in the eyes of others. However, over time Alison's mother witnessed both my mother's and step-father's treatment of me, so by the time this occurred she was more than clear on how my mother functioned. She decided she would call my dad and talk to him.

Alison's mom talked to my dad for a long time and explained that my mother had agreed to let me stay there. She convinced my dad that staying in Florida in the same school, with all my friends, would be the best thing for everyone involved, most of all me.

Dad finally agreed to let me stay, and my mother moved on with her life. I think my dad was a little hurt that I wanted to stay in Florida; I think he thought I didn't want to live with him. It had nothing to do with not wanting to live with him; I wanted to graduate high school in the same place I had grown up. What I didn't realize at the time was I was just beginning to discover my own place in the world and my life was just starting out.

I would later be surprised at all the things that changed and happened in just a few short months and how much those changes and the choices I made would effect the rest of my life.

Dad offered to send $100 each month, but he didn't really send it very often. Alison only remembers him sending one payment to her mother, but as they both tend to emphasize, they weren't looking for money, they just wanted to see me happy.

I felt obligated to pay my own way and even though Alison and I could always do extra stuff for her dad – like painting all of the ceilings in the house for extra money – I did not want to be a burden. Alison's family insisted that the only thing I needed to worry about was school, but I just didn't feel right about it, so I went out and found a job at Eckerd Drug Store.

I didn't have my own car and it was too far to walk, so I had to beg rides from other people. More often than not Alison would take me to work in her Jeep. This Jeep was the center of so many memories that we would create that year. Unfortunately, it was becoming more and more difficult to get the ride to work because Alison also had things she needed to do, so I had to quit. I wasn't happy about it, but the job was becoming more of a hassle for everyone than a help. There was no way I would be able to earn enough to get my own car with the limited hours I was able to work.

So, for the rest of the school year we did what normal teenage girls do during their senior year. The local golf course keeper knew the two of us by name because we would often sneak out at night and drive the Jeep across the course and jump the hills. He didn't seem all that bothered by it, but we knew that Alison's parents would never allow us to cause such trouble and put ourselves at risk. To cover up the evidence, we always went to the car wash before going home because her parents would inspect the Jeep for any signs of nonsense. I still don't know how we got away with this, but we certainly had a good deal of fun.

The last time I visited Alison we took the Jeep out for a ride again. We didn't go jumping hills on the local golf course, but we did take a little trip down memory lane again. Now Alison's young daughter wants the Jeep when she is old enough to drive; luckily they have quite a few years before Alison has to start worrying that her daughter will be out mudding in that Jeep. I do expect it will be inspected a bit more thoroughly than her parents did when we had it.

Sometime near the end of the school year we had the usual career day, which included local colleges and all branches of the military. I really had not given much thought to joining the military until that day. I listened to what everyone had to say, but I liked the presentation that the Air Force gave. They had a chart that showed where those who didn't go to college would be in four years, those who went to college, and those who joined the Air Force.

Those who didn't go to college would end up in a low-paying job more often than not, those in college would end up in debt and looking for a job, and those who joined the Air Force would be well trained in a career of their choice with decent pay and money for college if they wanted to go. In the Air Force, you didn't have to worry about the economy, lay-offs, and plant closings; you would have job security for as long as you wanted it. I also liked the fact that the Air Force had an easier basic training than other branches of the military. Everyone knows about the basic training for other branches of the military: sleeping in mud holes or cold barracks. The Air Force presents their basic training like a country club and said we would be staying in hotel-like rooms instead of barracks or tents. I liked that idea and started to think about it.

My dad had been in the Air Force, and I wanted him to be proud of me. This is something that I never heard from him and I desperately wanted his approval. I still wasn't sure that I could handle basic training, and even more so four years in any branch of the military. I decided to ask Alison's mom what she thought about it all.

"Do you think I can do it?" I asked her.

"Of course you can do it! You can do anything you set your mind to."

This woman not only believed in me, she believed in me completely. That was really all I needed to hear. I believed in her, so when she believed in me, I knew that I could do it. I doubt she knows how much of an impact she has had on my life and how much she changed it just by being there for me and believing in me when I wasn't so sure about myself. She loved me when she really had no reason in the world to care about me. She encouraged me the same way she encouraged Alison and she was always there when I needed someone. I am grateful to her every single day of my life for her love, encouragement, and for setting an example that I am proud to follow in my everyday life.

I graduated a few months later, and Alison's parents were sitting there as proud of me as they were of Alison. To this day my graduation photo is displayed in their home along with Alison's. Even though I barely made the grades I needed to pass, I did make it, I did graduate, and I was going out to start my own life. Never again would anyone else determine my fate. I was so proud of myself, I had shown everyone who said I would never amount to anything that I could at least graduate, and soon I was going to show them in an even bigger way.

After I went through all the testing and the Air Force determined I was fit to join, I began the paperwork process to begin my new life. I hadn't told any of my friends what I was planning and I had managed to keep it from everyone including Alison. I decided I would tell all of my friends at an AC/DC concert that we were planning to attend. When the day arrived I was a nervous wreck and I started drinking even before the concert. By the time we arrived I was pretty tipsy and I remember very little of that night. Alison has a clearer memory of that night.

"We were all there having a good time and then Jayme just blurted out that she was going to join the Air Force. We all thought she was joking at first, but she made it clear that she was very serious. We were all upset and tried to talk her out of it, but Jayme had made up her mind and there was no changing it."

Everyone, including Alison's mom, told me that I could stay. They told me they would help me apply for grants to college, and if I needed I could even stay with them. I didn't want to do that. I wanted to be on my own.

Alison's family had been very good to me; they took care of me when nobody else was there to do it and they helped me through a very rough time in my life. But I did not want to depend on anyone for a day longer than I had to. I loved them dearly and I knew they meant well, but I didn't want to be someone's charity case because they felt sorry for me or because I had no other options. I was tired of depending on other people. I had learned too many times in my life that depending on others only led to disappointment. Anyone that I had depended on in the past had let me down.

My mother was off living her own life; my dad had his own family and three children to put through private school. I knew he loved me, but I was not at the top of his priority list; he had a new family and I wasn't exactly a large part of that family. I didn't hold any anger or resentment about this. Both my dad and step-mom had always been good to me, but I also had not spent a great deal of time with them. There were a few times that my dad actually said that it was hard for him to love me when I was so far away from him.

I was alone, and if I didn't join the Air Force, I honestly did not see too many other options that wouldn't belittle or degrade me. There was a life that was available to me and I was going to go get it. The whole world was in front of me; I just didn't realize how big that world would become.

DARE, DREAM, DISCOVER

As I look back at this part of my life, I realize that Alison's mom had been a large factor in not only my survival, but also in who I would become. Reading a journal entry I recently wrote, I realize that without her I would not be where I am today:

Encouraging Words

Isn't it amazing how a few encouraging words from someone can actually change your life? The encouraging words that were spoken to me by my best friend's mother at the age of 18 really did change my life. I will never forget hearing those words when I asked her "Do you really think that I can do this?" She replied "Yes! You can do anything you set your mind to!" Well then, that was it, I believed in her and she believed in me. That was all of the confirmation that I needed.

In my mind, I was already in the Air Force at that moment without any doubts I knew that I could DO IT! I don't think that she realized what kind of effect those words would have on just me, but also to other people's lives that I have affected as a direct result of her belief in me and her kindness to me. She was the one who took me into her home after my mother left. She was the one who gave me lunch money for school. She proudly hung my graduation picture on her mantle along with the pictures of her other children. Wow, that still means a lot to me to this day. She is my Oprah Winfrey in life.

I was on a path destined to be a nobody in this life; God knows what would have happened to me if she was not there for me.

I have been put in situations in life to help other people because of her. Because of her kindness, I have been able to show kindness to other people in need and other families in need. It truly is a beautiful ripple effect, petals on a rose.

Let's not ever forget how we can truly change the course of the world with something as simple as encouraging words, acts of kindness, and just believing in the best for people. I am going to make an effort today and everyday to say at least one encouraging word to someone that comes across my path. I'm not perfect or high spirited everyday–yes I can be cynical and negative just like everyone else–

but I feel so much better and a sense of purpose in life when I can make a difference. I bet that my inspiration in life, my hero, had no idea that those few encouraging words would help me grow into the person that I am today.

I graduated basic training! I traveled the world! I helped a suffering family get into a home after a devastating war. I supported the efforts of many to get food and shelter to the earthquake victims in Pakistan. I always notice the hard labor workers in any country that I visit and work in; I appreciate them and try to give them as much spare change as I can. I challenge you to speak encouraging words to someone, especially a child full of hopes and dreams. That is our future, let's not discourage, let's encourage those around us!

* * *

As I look back at my childhood, I could spend the time feeling sorry for myself, but instead I prefer to look at it as a learning experience. I learned to be self-reliant. I learned that although life can be difficult, there is nothing that can't be overcome if you refuse to give up, even under the worst of circumstances. People often comment when they hear my story that they are surprised that I survived and still came out without ending up on drugs or worse. It never occurred to me to give up and drugs were never an option. I knew there was more to life and I wanted it. I have had to fight and claw every step of the way, but it never occurred to me that I couldn't do anything that I set my mind to.

Today I am estranged from my mother, but I don't hate her; in fact, I feel sorry for her because I know she is not happy with herself and I doubt she ever will know any true happiness in her life. I have accepted that she was and still is a person who has a great deal of pain in her life, most of which is probably self-inflicted, but I also know that there are some serious emotional issues that she suffers with. Unless she decides to get some help, she will always suffer from these problems.

Recently I discovered that writing in my journal and blogging are both very therapeutic for me. Getting the hurt and pain out, even if those that have hurt me will never hear the words, writing helps me move on and make peace with my past. One day when writing about my mother, this is what came to mind:

How can I not forgive you?

I don't want to hate you.

I don't want to live my life with bitterness in my heart.

I will not live my life reliving the past, blaming you or anyone in the family for my pain.

It was hard growing up with no love from you. Feeling your bitterness towards me, dealing with your mood swings, taking the blame for your misery, looking into your cold lifeless eyes; all of those things hurt and scared me.

Where were you when I needed a mother? Where were you for my first prom? Where were you when I had no money or food? Where were you when the electricity was shut off? Where were you on Christmas?

I didn't want all of the responsibility you gave me at such a young age. Having to watch after my newborn sister when I was only 6 years old; that was dangerous. I was a baby myself.

I don't understand how a mother can be so cruel. What did I do to deserve this?

I understand now that you have a sickness, but I did not understand then. You robbed me of a childhood.

I think part of the emptiness and loneliness that I constantly feel is not having any type of nurturing from you.

I think that is why I have a hard time with relationships. I don't know if I will ever be able to truly love someone and stay with them. I either end up pushing them away or I run away.

All I can do is move forward with my life and be the best person that I can be. I want to help other people in pain. I want to let them know that they can make something of their lives even if their parents abandoned them, abused them, and didn't love them. They still have a chance in life, and I'm going to be that person to let them know that their dreams and hopes in life are still possible.

CHAPTER VI

AIRMAN HARRIS

ALISON HAS A BLACK-AND-WHITE PHOTO OF ME DURING BASIC TRAINING. I'm in uniform and I'm holding a sign that says "I miss you sister." My hair is pulled back in typical military style for women with long hair and my lower lip is sticking out. I did miss Alison and all of my friends, I missed her mother's wisdom, and I even missed working with her dad, but I can't say that I really missed home; I wasn't homesick like the others.

Many would cry themselves to sleep at night and call home as often as possible. I would hear them tell their families that they wanted to go home and they hated it here. I wasn't home sick; I was relieved. I would never have to go back to my mother's house again, I never had to do what she told me to do, and I never again had to worry about relying on her or anyone else for my well being. I might have to scratch and claw every step of the way, but now the only person that I had to rely on was myself and I knew I could take care of myself; I had done it many times in the past.

AIRMAN HARRIS

Basic training wasn't the country club they had implied back in high school, but it wasn't horrible. I had survived 18 years of hell and arrived in the Air Force stronger than most of the others. The drill instructors thought I was some kind of princess because of my looks. I had no control over my looks and I had never assumed that I could get by based on the fact that I was pretty.

During the days of my movie star dreams, my dad made it clear that my looks were not going to pay the bills. "You aren't going to be a movie star; get a real job," he would tell me. "You aren't any prettier than the ugliest girl walking down the street. Don't ever do a job half-assed."

Those words stuck in my head. I believe my dad was proud of my choice to join the Air Force. Not just because I was following in his footsteps, but because I was taking control of my own life, my own destiny, and I was determined to make it.

For reasons that are still unknown to me, I arrived three days after most of the others for basic training. This made life difficult for me because I had no idea how I was supposed to stand, address people, and many other things. I found myself in trouble more often than not, even during meal time. The first meal I had in basic training I went and got my food and took two glasses of water. The next thing I knew, someone was barking in my ear, "Do you think you are special? Do you think you are better than everyone else that you only need two glasses of water?"

I was confused; I had no idea what was wrong with two glasses of water. I would later discover that, for hydration reasons, we were all required to have three glasses of water with each meal. From time to time, if someone was close enough and could whisper to me to let me know what I was supposed to be doing, I could figure out what I had to do to make things right, but more often than not I simply learned to hang back and follow what the others were doing.

Their yelling and screaming didn't bother me. I was used to that; I had been through so much worse growing up. I wasn't going to break down and cry, I wasn't going to quit, and I would never let anyone take my dreams away. I ended up doing a great many push-ups until I caught up. I also found myself getting the worst jobs possible. While others might get dorm chief duty, I would be the one who had to sweep under everyone's bed. I really didn't care; I wasn't afraid of hard work, and if I was going to sweep, I was going to sweep better than anyone else could. The physical work only made me physically stronger and my mental strength was unbreakable.

My drill instructor did not make any bones about her feelings toward me the day we had to wear our dress blues for pictures. Nobody was allowed to wear make-up at any time during basic training. On this day the drill sergeant decided to see if she could torture us.

"Anyone who wants to wear make-up has to get everything out of that closet and back in within five minutes." She was pointing to the closet where everyone from the dorm had their luggage from our arrival. Everything belonging to the twenty or more women that shared the dorm was crammed into that closet in any fashion that it might fit. I wanted to wear make-up for my picture, so, along with one other girl, I got all the luggage out of and back into that closet in the time allotted. When the drill sergeant realized that I had actually accomplished something she thought would never happen, she came up to me and said "I hate you." I didn't care. I got to wear make-up, and I showed her that she was not going to stand in my way of anything that I wanted.

I was determined to get through basic training and move on. The people that tried to scare me out of the Air Force and make my life hell had no idea what I had been through. They didn't know that they were nothing to me when I looked back at how I had grown up. They judged me on my blonde hair, blue eyes, and petite build, but they didn't know that underneath the fluffy exterior was a will of steel and a young woman who did not know how to quit.

While the other girls cried and called home, I dreamed of what the future might hold. I no longer wanted to be a movie star; instead I decided I was going to be a fire fighter. I had passed the tests for all kinds of clerical and mind-numbingly dull jobs, but I didn't want that kind of job. I wanted excitement, I wanted adventure, and I wanted something different from everyone else.

I barely passed the physical tests for the firefighters, but I wouldn't let that sway me or scare me away. The fact that I hadn't passed with flying colors only made me more determined to not only do the job, but do it better than anyone else. However, first I had to get through basic training.

When we were given our assignments for technical school, the drill instructor asked each of us what we were doing. She didn't say much about anyone until she got to me. When I told her I was going into firefighting she literally fell to the ground laughing at me. I suppose this was intended to sway me or scare me, it didn't. I had never asked for her opinion and I already knew what she thought of me. I would be a firefighter, and her insults and degrading comments only made me more determined to do well. If I gave up, it would make her right, but I knew she was wrong about me and I would prove it her.

It didn't matter to me if I ever crossed paths with her again or if she ever heard that I had passed my firefighting training; the only thing that mattered was that I knew she was wrong. The drill sergeant had a big surprise coming from this princess. It would not matter to me how much she screamed, yelled, or degraded me, I was not giving up. I had a place to sleep and food everyday, what else did I need?

DARE, DREAM, DISCOVER

I passed basic training. I wasn't at the top of the class, but I passed and was moving on to the next phase of my life. It was time for me to go into my firefighter training, and I was ready to go to tech school and begin my life as a firefighter.

The first day was a shock to both me and my classmates. I walked into the break room that first day and discovered I was the only woman in the place. The room that had been filled with chatter and laughter only a moment before went dead silent. The phrase "you could have heard a pin drop" fit that moment in a way that I have never seen before or since. Every man in that room turned to look at me, and I wanted to find someplace to hide. Suddenly being female made me very uncomfortable. If I could have morphed into a man in that instant; I would have, no second thoughts. I was actually embarrassed that I was a woman, and they seemed to be more than a little surprised as well.

It never occurred to me to quit or find a different profession. I was going to be a Fire Dawg even if that meant that I was the only female one in history. I would show them all that even if I was barely 110 pounds that

Airman Harris

I could hang with the big "Dawgs," and I was not going to be sitting on the porch while they were out chasing adventure.

The training was not easy. It was both physically and mentally challenging. I would go to bed at night completely exhausted. My body ached and my mind never quit. I could hear my instructor in my sleep: "Move faster! What, you can't pick that up? What are you going to do when there is a real person inside of a real fire? Is someone going to die because you can't do your job?" But I wasn't going to quit; I would do whatever I had to do to pass this training. I would become a firefighter and be a damn good one.

I found myself as a part of a new kind of family in tech school. Being the only woman, I was not sure what to expect, but my classmates accepted me and were my greatest cheerleaders. I believe that if not for those men pushing me, I would have washed back and had to go through the training all over again, but they wanted me to get through and pass as much as I did. I did struggle, especially with some of the physical aspects of the training, but I never gave up and I always had the guys encouraging me to keep going.

DARE, DREAM, DISCOVER

When all was said and done, I passed. A full bird Colonel came up to me after graduation and said that he had heard about me and that many didn't think I would make it. He told me "good job," which at the time was the highest compliment any graduate could hope for. I did do a good job and I was proud of myself.

I remember having anxiety attacks before graduation. I knew I was going to be stationed at Eglin Air Force Base in Florida and I was really scared. I was told that Eglin was the largest and busiest Air Force Base including the fire department world wide.

I like challenges, but in addition to the anxiety of entering a new environment and living with a bunch of men 24hours every other day, I was told that Eglin was one of the most physically and mentally challenging places to work. We had to train on every aircraft for the armed services, and Eglin was also a back-up site for the space shuttle landings. The firefighters were extra tough there. One of my instructors had been stationed at Eglin at one time, and he would give me little pep talks.

"It's not like anyone is going to yell 'bunker drill' the moment you walk in the door. You are going to do just fine." He once told me that if I could make it at Eglin, I could make it anywhere. I really didn't understand what that meant until I arrived at Eglin. Sometimes I wonder if my instructor knew what I was about to face in the next phase of my young life. Nothing that I had learned during tech school prepared me for what was to come.

CHAPTER VII

EGLIN AIR FORCE BASE, FLORIDA

DARE, DREAM, DISCOVER

DURING MY BREAK FROM TECHNICAL SCHOOL, I SPENT SOME TIME VISITING ALISON AND THE GUY WHO HAD BEEN MY BOYFRIEND SINCE NINTH GRADE. Then I took the longest bus ride of my life. I had to take a Greyhound bus from central Florida to the panhandle, which is normally a six- or seven-hour journey, but this trip took about thirteen hours. We must have hit every bus stop possible, and it seemed as if every weird person in the world piled onto this bus. We were able to walk around and take breaks at the bus stations, and I remember watching people; so many were behaving strangely and some simply scared me. As we neared my new home, I gazed through the bus windows at my new surroundings in Destin and Fort Walton Beach, Florida.

When I finally reached the Ft. Walton Greyhound bus station around midnight, another female firefighter was there to pick me up. I didn't realize it at the time, but she would be the cause of some hard times for me. She had gotten there about six months ahead of me and had been injured on duty. When I got there she was working in an administrative position in the alarm room. She would be one of the reasons I would be judged so harshly upon my arrival, simply because we were both women.

She drove me to Eglin Air Base and dropped me off at the temporary billeting accommodations; I would start my in-processing the next day. The weather in the panhandle was extremely cold compared to central Florida; I never liked the cold weather. Looking back, the chill in the air would be very telling of the days to come for me.

Arriving at Eglin Air Force Base, I was a little nervous, but I was also anxious to get on with my life. The reception I received was not exactly cold, but it was rather strained. These men had dealt with other women in the past, and their experience was obviously not something they wanted to repeat. I don't believe anyone ever judged me solely on my looks, but they did judge me based on my gender. They made assumptions about me as an individual without getting to know me, without asking any questions, and without taking the time to see what I might do; they simply decided I was going to fail without ever giving me a chance.

DARE, DREAM, DISCOVER

I was often reminded of the women before me: one had been there for a short time and ended up injured, another had gotten pregnant within six months, and they expected one or the other from me. It was made clear to me that they believed I would be in an administrative position in a very short period of time.

I was told I would have to work twice as hard and do twice as well as everyone else just to be considered equal, so I did work hard: The way things worked with this department, and probably in most fire departments anywhere, is that the new person gets to do all of the menial stuff the other guys don't want to do.

While someone was normally assigned to cook dinner, we usually sent someone out to get lunch, and of course that someone would be me. That wasn't bad, but other tasks were physically demanding. For example, filling the water coolers was hard work. The water coolers were huge; it seemed to me like they were at least three feet tall. It had a handle on each side near the top, but it was very heavy. I had to offload the old one from the fire truck from the last shift. Just reaching it and getting it off the truck was hard enough, but then I had to empty the water and refill it with fresh ice and water from the garden hose faucet, and then carry it back to the truck and secure it with a bungee cord to the truck again. I never asked for help because the last thing I wanted was for anyone to think I was a sissy or that I couldn't do the job.

While this form of hazing generally lasts for a couple of weeks for most new people, mine lasted about six months. I was run through more bunker drills than I could ever imagine and every possible kind of extra training anyone could think up. I know they were trying to chase me off and make me give up, but again I refused to be bullied into giving up on something I wanted. It would eventually get better, and when I was able to look back, I realized all of those things simply made me a better firefighter and a stronger person both physically and mentally.

The biggest issue for the men seemed to be the fact that certain things had to change with me there. I had separate quarters from everyone else, which ended up being a room that a battalion chief would have. The room was only a few feet bigger than the others, and I had a private shower, but some of the men resented this. There were a few who were bothered by the fact that they couldn't walk around naked anymore, but some found that to be a good thing. Some would laugh and remind the others they didn't normally walk around naked anyway and also reminded them that they really weren't that interested in seeing them naked as it was. Working out was a bit of a hassle as well; we were required to work out, and I had to work out in the men's bathroom/shower area. This meant I could only work out during certain times of the day, and I had to put a sign on the door to let them know there was a female on the premises. While these arrangements worked most of the time, there were rare occasions that I would find one of my co-workers coming out of the shower stark naked during my workout. I would simply say "Hi" and get on with my workout, and they would go on and get dressed. Nobody ever made a big deal of it, as accidents do happen to everyone at some point.

As time went by, I found my own niche within this very tight-knit group of men. A firehouse is a family; they spend more time with one another than even their own families. More often than not holidays were spent together, even if it was our day off, because that was our family.

Upon arriving at the firehouse I discovered that dinner meant you either brought your own or you were part of a cooking group that usually fixed something along the lines of Hamburger Helper. As time went by, I learned to cook, and the guys discovered they liked eating what I cooked. I soon became the person that cooked all of the meals around the firehouse. The men devoured my meals and I took pride in doing something that they all seemed to greatly appreciate. No longer did we have Hamburger Helper, instead we would have ribs, chicken, or whatever sounded good, with all the trimmings. Of course, cooking for 16 firefighters is a bit different than cooking for myself, and even now I still tend to make enough for an entire battalion when I cook.

One man in particular made a lasting impression on me. Mr. Harris was one of my supervisors and Station Chief. He never let me believe that I was anything but the best. He would remind me that I had a name to live up to; since his name was also Harris, I was not allowed to do anything but bring pride to that name.

Mr. Harris was never easy on me, but he was never unfair. He demanded a great deal from me because he knew that I was capable; he was never going to let me slack off and give the people that were criticizing me the satisfaction of being right. The men respected him and

I adored him; in many ways I felt as if he had become my surrogate father. There were times I would lash out at him because I felt he was being unfair or too hard on me. I was pretty defensive during those days, and I now realize he was simply trying to make me the best I could be. To this day I have a problem with being defensive with people. It is not a trait that I like, but it stems from the fire days when I had to fend for myself and protect my name and reputation.

He knew I was capable and he refused to accept anything but my best. If I was sick, he would tell me that I needed to go to the hospital if I was too sick to work. I didn't always appreciate his way of doing things, but in the end he was doing what was best for me.

Mr. Harris taught me to play pinochle, a card game with him and some of the other senior firefighters; it wasn't long before I was able to actually beat him in a game. I was quite proud of myself, but Mr. Harris, whom I believe was secretly pleased that he had taught me so well, refused to show any of it. Instead, he kind of growled at me with his lip turned up and walked away. I was a bit cocky about all of it, which is probably why he reacted the way he did, but I know he was proud of me that night. Coincidently, my dad was a big pinochle fan and player. Later I would go on to play against my father, and I know that it made my dad proud to have his daughter play the game.

Mr. Harris was always there when I needed him, even if he didn't realize how much his voice rooting me on during drills would make me push harder. I wasn't going to let down the one person that believed in me; I would show him he was right in his belief or I would die trying. The other men would either laugh at me or make bets that I would fail, but Mr. Harris was always there rooting for me and giving me that extra push that I needed.

Very few people could get through the protective barrier I had built around myself, but Mr. Harris never let that stop him; he got through all of it and managed his way into my heart.

I loved him like a father, and I believe he loved me like a daughter. Many times I would catch him grinning his approval when I did well. He never said much, but that grin told me all I needed to know. He loved his family more than anything in the world. I loved to sit and listen as he talked about his children; he was a loving and proud father. He described his wife as being about my size and quite the spitfire. I could hear it in his voice when he spoke of her; he loved her more than anything in the world. Sometimes, when he would speak of her, I would wonder if I would ever have that kind of love from someone.

I would go on to be recognized as Airman Below The Zone, which gave me my third stripe early. This put me at E-4 rank and gave me extra pay. I was so proud that I had accomplished this goal, but it was dampened a bit by knowing the person that I had gone up against. We had been friends all along and were neck and neck for this promotion, but in the end I did better, so I was the one promoted. My friend then went around telling others that I only got it because I was female. To make matters worse, most of the others agreed with him. I knew I had earned everything I had gotten, so the assumption that I had been promoted based on anything but hard work cut me like a knife.

For this reason and so many like it, at the end of my four years when my enlistment was up, I decided it was time to move on. I was tired of fighting, I was tired of working my butt off only to be over looked for other promotions, and I was tired of being accused of having things handed to me because I was a woman. I knew better, and I believe deep down they knew better, but for reasons of their own they would never admit that I had earned everything that I had while I was there.

After my discharge, I decided to go to vocational school. I had the GI bill from the Air Force, and it seemed like a good idea to take advantage of it. It was a strange transition for me. I had gone from having medical insurance and many benefits to no medical coverage and minimum wage; I was working part time as a waitress and surviving off of the tips. I certainly wasn't living it up, but I was getting by, and for the time being that was good enough.

About a year after I left the Air Force I got a phone call that changed everything for me.

"Jayme, is that you?" the voice on the other end inquired. The voice turned out to be one of the firefighters from Eglin.

"We didn't know if you were still in town or not, but I need to tell that Mr. Harris has passed away."

My heart began pounding and my head was spinning.

How could this have happened? He was young; I was sure it must have been a heart attack or a fire. What else could it be? But the person on the other end said something that pulled the rug out from under me.

"He committed suicide...his eight-year-old son found him." I have no memory of what I said or how I responded to the rest of the conversation; I was in a state of shock. Never again would anyone know the blessing of having this man as their champion or what it felt like to have him believe in you or see that grin that let them know he was proud of them. I would never have the chance for these things either.

One of the few people in this world that loved me for me and believed in me was gone, and I never had the chance to tell him how much he had meant to me. My friend invited me to the funeral and offered to come and pick me up; we could go to the funeral together. I accepted his invitation and was grateful for the ride.

At the funeral in Mr. Harris' hometown of Pensacola, Florida, I remember crying so hard that my chest was heaving. I was trying to contain it; I knew I was making a scene, but I couldn't help myself. My heart was breaking and I didn't know what to do to make it better. People were turning around and staring, wondering who I was. I had never met his wife face to face, so she had to be wondering who I was being that I was completely hysterical at her husband's funeral. I couldn't understand how the man that had taught me to be so strong in the face of any adversity had made the choice to do this.

I knew how much stress came from being a firefighter, and Mr. Harris had been promoted several times. With each promotion came more responsibility and the need to use computers. Mr. Harris was happy to do paperwork, but he much preferred to do it on paper. I can only think that the stress took its toll, and he was not the kind of man who would burden others with his problems, so he just sucked it all in until it became too much for him.

I watched through my tears as my fellow firefighters carried his coffin out of the church. They were greeted by a 102' ladder truck parked out front with an American flag at the top swaying in the wind. I stood in the cemetery as the bagpipes played and someone handed his son his old helmet. Each thing that happened that day only increased my pain; I didn't know if it would ever stop, but I knew that I couldn't take much more.

DARE, DREAM, DISCOVER

After finding enough strength to go to the reception hall, I was introduced to his wife for the first time. I will never forget her words, "Oh yes, you are the one that he would always come home and talk about; he called you 'his daughter.' I could not hold it together after hearing those words. I truly loved that man like a father figure. Just like I owed Alison's mom credit for believing in me, I owed this man credit for giving me strength.

I couldn't have made it without someone believing in me from the fire department; I just needed to know that one person thought that I could do it. Mr. Harris always believed in me. For me the world would never be the same with him gone.

The guys from the fire department included me in everything and invited me out for a couple of drinks at the local firefighter-themed bar called "Hosers." We sat there and talked about our memories of being newbies in the fire department and of Mr. Harris and how he would scare the living daylights out of all of us, but how he still made us laugh and always made us proud to be firefighters at the same time. I began to realize this was really the only family I had ever truly had, no matter how dysfunctional. When it came right down to it, we took care of our own and we stuck together. Those were the men that were getting me through the pain. I suddenly realized in that moment that those men respected me and they considered me a part of their family as well. For the first time in my life, I felt that I was a part of something and felt like I belonged and was needed.

The Fire Chief and most of my ex-military firefighter friends were trying to convince me to come back and work as a civilian with the rest of them. Eglin's fire department employs both military and civil service employees, and most of the guys I had worked with were now in civil service. They wanted me to come back?

Maybe they realized that I was a firefighter and that my sex didn't matter. It had never occurred to me before to even consider civil service or going back to the fire department, but at that time more than ever, I felt that I was accepted and would be welcomed back. I could be a part of this family once again. Also, by going back, I would start out at an annual salary of over $30,000, which was a lot more than getting by on minimum wage and tips. I applied and soon would end up where things all started for me: Eglin Air Force Base.

I learned a great deal in the time I spent at Eglin, and while some was good, much of it was about how prejudice can warp a person's thinking and make life for the person they are biased against a living hell. I am sure I could have brought legal charges against those I worked with, but I didn't see the point. It was more important to me to show them that they were wrong for making assumptions based on my sex or the way I looked.

Before these men ever met me, some had made assumptions solely because I was a woman. Some did everything in their power to make me want to quit, give up, and question myself. I can't say that there weren't days when it would have been easier just to ditch it all and find something else to do, but it never occurred to me that I would do anything but be the best firefighter they had ever seen, male or female. This was really my first taste of discrimination, and I knew that pressing legal charges would only make things worse; I wanted their respect not a court battle.

As I look back, I probably did earn their respect, but most of them would have rather quit themselves than admit that I was good at what I did. It really doesn't matter that much to me now, as I know what I did, I know that I never gave up, and I also know that my experience with discrimination would profoundly effect me for the rest of my life. I didn't realize it then, but that time made me a more compassionate person. It also taught me to look at the person versus the stereotype. Often that has caused me to be attacked verbally for my views, but I would rather stand up for the person that is being hurt for no reason rather than be ignorant and bias as the person who simply stands by and keeps their mouth shut in order to go along with the crowd.

*   *   *

Memories of You

I can't believe you are gone. The way you decided to end your life came as a shock to all who knew you. You were one of the few people who believed in me and supported me. When most wanted to see me fail, you helped me to succeed.

I saw you as the strongest person in the world; most were intimidated by your mere presence. Everyone looked up to you and admired you. To have you on my side meant a lot, you weren't just anyone ... you were Mr. Harris ... a well respected name and figure in the Fire Department. I will remember you forever.

The hardest thing in my life was attending your funeral and memorial service and seeing your wife and kids have to say their final good byes and pay their last respects. Seeing your son reach out to accept your old fire helmet from my fellow firefighters was gut wrenching to say the least.

If anything positive can be said about this it is that I would have never have gone back to the fire department without this tragic event bringing me close to the only family that I have ever felt a true part of ... "my fire dawg family."

They are the ones who got me through the pain and heartache of losing you and knowing for the first time what it felt like to belong to a family who cared about my well being and wanted me back into their lives again. They needed me too ... wow... that is hard to believe, someone needed me for the first time ... they missed my cooking and me being there

AIRMAN HARRIS

for them to lift them up, maybe this blue eyed blonde girl that most judged by her exterior finally made a difference in other people's lives not based on my looks but for the person that I was.

Mr. Harris, you will always be a part of me. Thank you for molding me into the person that I am today. You have given me the toughness and strength that is needed to overcome the overwhelming obstacles in life.

CHAPTER VIII

CIVIL SERVICE DAYS

GOING BACK INTO THE FIRE DEPARTMENT AS A CIVIL SERVANT WAS MUCH BETTER, BUT I STILL FACED SOME OF THE SAME CHALLENGES AS BEFORE. In addition, this time I was making a lot more money than the military guys were and I was their boss now. Talk about friction! I started my civil service career as a supervisor. My GS-6 rank was higher than a 4-stripe staff sergeant, and some argued that my rank was equal to a 5-stripe tech sergeant. I had to write military performance appraisals and decoration recommendations for the airmen that I supervised. I got more respect in this position, but not from everyone.

I was still working harder than anyone in my position and a few levels higher. While most supervisors did paperwork in the day and took it easy, I was still getting my hands dirty training right along with the new recruits. I wanted to show everyone that I was not one to just give orders and otherwise not participate; I would be seen as lazy if I acted like any of my peer supervisors. I would train all day and do my supervisor and crew chief reports at night. Getting to bed before midnight was a luxury, as more often than not I usually wasn't in bed until long after midnight. We had to wake up at 5:30 each morning when going off shift to wash the trucks and have the station clean for the next arriving shift.

It didn't matter what I did, how hard I worked, or even how good that work might have been, I could not win with most people and learned very quickly that my hard work did not pay off. I was passed over for promotion the first three times because my shift assistant fire chief stated that he was receiving pressure from everyone that he knew. There was talk that I would get promoted based only on the fact that I was a woman. I guess they didn't review my work records; they obviously had never been around while I was working. But in this case my work did not matter; I was a woman and that was all that mattered to the people who opposed me.

I knew I had earned my previous promotions and so did my chief, but that didn't change a thing. It felt to me like the other supervisors were playing a psychological game with the chief's head, and he was stupid enough to take the bait. I was working my butt off while they were sitting back taking it easy and just getting by, but they would still end up getting the promotions.

Meanwhile, I was left behind carrying the work load of what felt like five people. I was in charge of the fire department newsletter, I did off-duty charity work, and trained all new drivers on the ladder truck since I was the only one qualified on my shift to do the training for this truck. Additionally, I had my upgrade training to do: hazmat training, fire officer training, and fire instructor training, all of which were official Department of Defense (DOD) training classes that earned DOD certificates after passing. I had to take strenuous tests, both written and practical, and I passed them all. The more they tried to beat me down, the more determined I became to show them that I was the best damn firefighter out there, with or without promotions. They were not going to intimidate me or keep me down, and I would do whatever it took to prove myself. I didn't expect to prove anything to them, as I had become accustomed to their backward attitude about women, but I still had something to prove to myself. Letting myself down was never an option.

CIVIL SERVICE DAYS

After raising hell about getting passed over, I finally got promoted, but the stigma was still there. Again there was talk about the promotion being based on the fact that I was a woman, and many even went as far as to say they had given me the promotion simply to shut me up. However, I started to make a little headway, and I soon started winning awards such as Civilian of the Quarter and Civilian of the Year in the Fire Department, all for my actions in being first in response and putting out a fire on an F-16 fighter aircraft and saving the life of a pilot.

In addition to the battles that I faced, I could not stand the negativity that went on in the department. Some of the older civil service employees seemed down right miserable with their lives and work. I pictured myself in their shoes and close to retirement; I didn't want to be some gray-haired woman sitting around complaining about her life and career.

I knew there were better things out there. Would I be gray-haired and still proving myself to the non-believers? I had friends that were working in Hungary as firefighters as government contractors. They were making between $80,000 and $100,000 a year, and up to $80,000 was tax-free. They would call the fire station every now and then and tell us about job openings.

I finally decided to apply for these positions, but I turned down acceptance offers about five times. I wasn't quite ready to make the change.

I think the final turning point for me was 9/11. I wanted to be a part of something bigger than Eglin. I will never forget what I went through on that tragic day. I had just gotten off shift and arrived home. I turned on the television to see that a plane had just crashed into the World Trade Center.

Red flags went up in my head, but I was still confused as I tried to figure out what had just happened. I kept watching. When I saw the second plane crash into Tower Two, I immediately knew this was an act of terrorism. I had been through plenty of Response to Terrorism classes, and even got a few certificates on these types of events.

I'm sure not many people were thinking the same thoughts that I was on this day. I started to think about the firefighters that were responding to this emergency. I started to see more and more firefighters arrive on scene, and I was hearing reports of the hundreds of firefighters that were in the building when suddenly it began to collapse. At that moment, I could only think of one other time I felt sadness about a fellow firefighter dying: Mr. Harris.

This event made that seem almost insignificant in the overall scheme of things; I suddenly felt the loss of over 300 fellow firefighters, the loss of "my family." Words will never be able to express the sorrow in my heart that day, not only for my fellow firefighters, but for the innocent civilians and for my country. My head was spinning, my heart was pounding, and I was scared.

Then something happened that nobody in the United States could even imagine: a plane hit the Pentagon. All I could do was ask myself what the hell was going on? This attack was a sucker punch, an act of war. I was livid at such a cowardly act. In that instant I wanted to be in the military again, I wanted to fight for my country.

I was determined to not let this day, event, or memory of the lost lives ever escape my mind or life. This event also re-confirmed how, even though the fire department had its negative points, they were my family and nothing would ever change that.

DARE, DREAM, DISCOVER

Between the acts of 9/11, the negativity and hopeless that I felt in the fire department at Eglin, and not to mention the tax burden in my life, I was finally ready for a change. I accepted the position that I had turned down so many times before.

Every time I brought this up to others in the past they would tell me not to throw my career away and my boyfriends would beg me not to leave them. As I look back now, I realize that the other times simply were not the right time for me. Waiting for the right time would prove to be my best choice, and things would turn out exactly as they were meant to be in the long run.

I gave my shift assistant chief two weeks notice after accepting my new job. I was told that I was throwing away my retirement and that I was in line to be the next and only female fire chief at Eglin. Was I crazy? I was asked that many times.

No, I wasn't crazy, and while I probably was in line for that promotion, I can't say they would have promoted me without making me fight with all I had to get it. These people that treated me like a lesser person instead of their equal while I was there suddenly seemed shocked that I might not want to spend my life scratching and clawing for everything that I had earned. They tried talking me out of leaving, but I had my mind made up, and like every other thing that I have made my mind up to do in my life, nothing or nobody could change my course.

There was a little bit of a risk because I had to resign before I took my physical, which meant if I failed I would be out of work and unemployed. I had to go to Houston, Texas for my physical and background check. They tested for all kind of things, and many people did not pass simply because of a white blood cell imbalance or other uncommon blood disorder. About 10-15% of people do not pass these physicals for one reason or another, but I was willing to take the risk.

I have learned that nothing is gained in life by playing it safe and never taking risks to get ahead in life. I passed all of the tests and I was able to move on to the next phase of my life; my risks paid off and I have never looked back since.

Going to Kosovo was one of the greatest experiences of my life: I never knew that the smile of a little girl from Kosovo would change my life and heart forever.

DARE, DREAM, DISCOVER

***Journal Entry regarding my last thoughts on the
Fire Department:***

*I was told it is called Sexual Harassment: I call
it Hate. I have never been a fan of PC terms and
labeling the actions of others. If they are fair, call
them fair; if they are hateful, call it like it is! There
is no need for fancy terminology.*

*When I entered the fire department at the age of
19, I faced many challenges. Besides being 5'2" and
110 pounds, I entered a work environment where
99% of the people hated my guts, and they were not
afraid to tell me or to show me on a daily basis.*

*Some of the first words that I heard upon meeting
my new co-workers were: "You will have to work
twice as hard as any guy around here and make
higher scores on all of your tests, just to be seen
as equal." That would come from a guy who
actually stood up for me. Some of the other words of
encouragement were: "You will either be pregnant
in 6 months or put in an administrative position."*

*"You will never drive a fire truck. That has never
been done by a woman in this department and it*

116

sure isn't happening with you."

Besides all of the great words of encouragement, I also had tricks played on me like putting dead roaches on my pillow, people banging on my wall and doors at all hours of the night, and just about any form of humiliation you can think of on a daily basis. I was also forced to drill and train harder and longer than any other newcomer in the fire department as a means of trying to break me down. Guess what? It made me better!

I was told by my fire chief after nine years of being in the fire department that he could not promote me even though he knew I deserved it because all the guys would say I got promoted just because I was a female. I could go on and on, but I won't. I just found it difficult to understand what I did to deserve so much hate from another group of human beings.

99% of the time, I would win people over with my work ethic, and when they got to know the real person that I was, they would come around. But people would rotate out a lot and I would be forced to once again prove myself.

My seniority or time in service didn't matter. I could not ever let my guard down or ever act like other men in my position that were supervisors, because I would be seen as lazy. Even though I had to do reports and appraisals till all hours of the night, most supervisors did this while I was out training and proving how tough I was and proving that I deserved to be there.

I choose to look back on the good experiences and lessons that I learned in my eleven years of the fire department.

It is hard to describe what hate feels like. I could never understand why I was judged so harshly just because of their limited exposure or bad experiences with other women in the Fire Service.

Most just heard how horrible it was to work with women and that working with women will get them fired. Instead of a warm introduction, I got cold stares, rolling of eyes, and backs turned on me.

All I wanted was for people to give me a chance instead of stereotyping me from the beginning. I never got that chance after eleven years. But what I took away was far better than any of their acceptance towards me. I'm a survivor. I knew that after overcoming every challenge they placed in front of me on a daily basis for eleven years that I could do anything in life. Guess what; I was right.

FYI, a few accomplishments of mine in the Fire Service: Airman Below the Zone, first female driver of the first responding structural engine company, first female crew chief, first female ladder driver (47ft long with a 102' aerial), first female ladder driver certifier, first female ladder crew chief, first female battalion chief, first female fire department civilian of the quarter, first female fire department civilian of the year.

They can go on living their miserable lives filled with hate and prejudice; I've moved on to so many things, better things that I hope to share with others.

CHAPTER IX

KOSOVO AND KBR

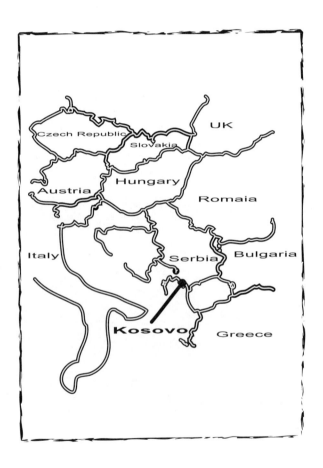

KOSOVO AND KBR

Upon being officially hired by KBR (Kellogg Brown and Root, the engineering and construction subsidiary of Halliburton), my first assignment was not exactly what I had wanted it to be. I had hoped to be sent to Hungary, where some of the other firefighters that I knew from Eglin were stationed, but that was a tough assignment to get. In Hungary the work wasn't as bad as some other places I could be assigned, and the living conditions were better than most of the other locations. Instead I found myself assigned to Kosovo, living on a US Army camp by the name of Camp Bondsteel.

I really had no idea what to expect while working in Kosovo. I knew very little about the war going on there, I didn't know much about their culture, and I did very little research before I left. Even if I had spent some time researching the country, it's very unlikely anything could have prepared me for what I would encounter when I arrived in Kosovo. I also could never have imagined the way this country and its people would change me in the short time I was there.

The war in Kosovo began when Yugoslav President Slobodan Milosevic set forth on a plan to ethnically cleanse Serbia. Ethnic cleansing included killing the Albanians, most of whom were Muslim, which did not coincide with Milosevic's Christian beliefs. Sending his troops into Kosovo, the Serbians began the slow and violent task of getting rid of the Albanians. Even after NATO entered into this conflict and attempted to find a solution, the genocide did not stop.

Even now after many years of fighting, the Albanian people are not entirely safe and they live in conditions that are below poverty with little hope or opportunity for anything more than the meager life they have. I found myself on a military installation that was somewhat similar to the life I had become accustomed to at Eglin. It also helped to have a couple of firefighters there that I already knew. I believe having a few familiar faces around made it easier for me to go into a strange country.

I was to be the crew chief in this fire department, and I soon discovered that what I had dealt with in the

KOSOVO AND KBR

Air Force and my civil service days would be nothing compared to the attitude I would face from the locals that worked with me. This is a country where women seldom worked outside of the home and the men were used to being the boss; they most certainly were not accustomed to taking orders from women.

I knew that if I had any hope of getting the job done and earning the respect of these men that I would have to be tough. I had to let them know from the very beginning that I would not accept anything less than the best they could possibly do, and just because I was a woman did not mean that I was any different than them when it came to hard work.

I think I surprised them with my attitude. I had to be very tough from the very beginning so they would respect my authority. I was being paid to train them to US fire department standards and that was not an easy task, not just because I was a female, but because of the strenuous work involved, the language barrier, and the cultural differences. Additionally, at no time could I show favoritism to either the Albanians or Serbians, or even be perceived to be giving anyone special treatment.

DARE, DREAM, DISCOVER

The Albanians worked in harmony with the Serbians for the most part, but both often displayed what I took as jealousy for one another. I can understand how each was proud of their nationality, and they had to follow certain rules to be employed on camp, such as staying away from religious and political discussions, etc. It was a very sensitive issue. While training and living together 24 hours every other day in a strenuous work environment, it is easy to lose your temper and patience with other people in general.

I had to train the Serbian and Albanians to Department of Defense standards and certification for firefighters. There were different levels of certification: Firefighter I, Firefighter II, Airport Firefighter I and II, Fire Inspector, Fire Officer, and Hazmat. We had to work every day and all day long. We were in our bunker gear with air pack almost all day everyday (full bunker gear weighs 40 pounds). We had to use the live burn house for training in the different techniques for putting out structural fires, and the trainers had to go in more times than the recruits. It was extremely hot in the burn houses. I went through several fire helmets during that period of time because my helmet and face shield would melt from being exposed for long periods of time in the heat. We also had to use the Fire Pit, which was a mock aircraft with a walk-in cockpit, for training them in extinguishing aircraft fires and rescuing aircrew.

We had to train the recruits to drive fire trucks: both structural fire trucks for building fires and emergencies, and crash fire trucks for the aircraft fires and emergencies. We had to train them on various techniques on using all fire department tools and equipment as well as working the pump panel on the fire trucks to deliver the right amount of water pressure.

Both the Albanians and Serbians were only allowed to speak English so that they would learn and be able to communicate at the fire scene in a common language. I was so impressed by how quickly they adapted to our language, both written and spoken. At the end of most days my head would hurt and my body ached, I was emotionally and physically exhausted.

The Albanians did not seem as strong-minded as the Serbians; the Albanians seemed more docile and displayed characteristics of years of oppression. But all of these guys came from a background where women do not work and the men are seen as providers and stronger and smarter than women. I can remember so many times that I would be carrying heavy stuff around and the guys would come up to me and take it out of my hand and give me a look like "you should not be carrying this." These guys had no idea what I went through at Eglin, having to prove myself and my strength to everyone.

It really shocked me to see that there were a few Albanian and Serbian women in this department – they were tough as nails.

As a supervisor and crew chief, I was in charge of an American driver and local nationals (Albanian and Serbian) on the back of the truck. I was in charge of directing everyone at the scene of an emergency. So, I still had to deal with the difficulty some Americans had accepting my authority right off the bat. At most departments around the world, it is rare to see a woman crew chief and woman driver; women are normally in the back of the truck or in administrative positions. The numbers are growing with women in non-traditional roles, but it will take time for women to not stick out like a sore thumb in most departments.

KOSOVO AND KBR

The Americans that were in the Kosovo Fire Department were the best of the best. It takes a strong person to leave the US and to endure the strenuous working conditions of being a contract firefighter. We were on a tough work schedule. We were not allowed to stop working until 10pm every night. We only had two or three 15-minute breaks throughout the day, lunch was 30 minutes, and dinner was 30 minutes. We were constantly training the local nationals, and we had to go to the gym every shift to work out. We had to administer written tests on the computer that came directly from the US that were DOD standards. So each night from around 9pm up until midnight we were administering the tests and having study time with the local nationals.

We also had to train them on operating the Alarm/Dispatch room, which is similar to being a 9-1-1 operator taking emergency information, reporting emergencies, dispatching the fire crews to the scene of accidents, and taking down the entire fire incident, etc.

Everyday we conducted live training drills on various buildings on camp and with various aircraft on the flight line. These drills were elaborate; I remember one in the base theatre in which they set up a smoke machine and had real people laying on the ground as mock victims. They would set things on fire around the building to simulate burning unexploded bombs and other objects. The mock victims had fake blood on them and had stickers on their chest indicating what kind of injuries they had. We had to respond, identify terrorist activity, extinguish fires, and pull people out of the building and treat their injuries. We did the same thing with the aircraft; we had to pull live people out. This work was exhausting on top of all of the other training and responsibilities.

Thanksgiving and Christmas were spent outside in the cold with our bunker gear on training the local nationals; we would get dirty and grimy training all day, and at mealtime we ate soggy sandwiches with dirty hands. I always smelled of smoke and soot; I had to scrub so hard to get the smoke smell off of me at the end of the day.

After a while the guys saw how hard I worked, how much I truly cared about them, and how much I wanted to see them succeed and get their certifications. They came around, just like everyone always does, but, like everywhere else, there were a couple of men who would be a constant thorn in my side. I often felt that this was like raising a difficult child. It was just like Eglin; we were all still a family at the end of the day, we were the ones who protected each other when in danger or in a burning building, and we depended on each other for our lives. There is a bond that forms with that, a bond that will never be broken or duplicated by any other event or person that comes into your life.

In the beginning I worked every other day. On our days off, many of the people that we worked with would take us to their villages and homes. There we would eat with their families. Dinner in Kosovo is not like dinner in the US; they don't rush through the meal. First we would have tea, then more drinks and talk for hours, after that we would finally eat dinner! The entire process took several hours, and although these people were very poor and had very little, they were always willing to share with us.

Kosovo was really the first time that I had been outside of the US for an extended time. I had only been to Egypt for two weeks while I was in the Air force, London for one month in the Air Force, Jamaica on vacation, and Mexico on vacation. On my first trip to Kosovo, I worked three months straight and took my first 10-day vacation in

Switzerland, then worked another three months before I had another vacation, which I used to return to the states. I had been gone over six months from the US and I was the most homesick I had ever been in my life. I used to think of the Atlanta International Airport as horrendous! When I landed there and was back on US soil, I literally wanted to kiss the ground.

The people seemed more friendly than usual and the US seemed more civilized to me than ever. Having been in a war-torn country where people had to fight for their life to survive, it made me really appreciate how good I had it and how lucky I was to be a US citizen.

At first being in Kosovo rubbed me the wrong way due to the culture shock; I detested the pushing and shoving and what seemed to me like the rudeness of most people there. It seemed they didn't understand the importance of personal space; waiting in lines seemed to be a shoving match, and I was beginning to find it really annoying.

People stared a lot, and not just at me; it happened with all of my American co-workers when we were out on the town or traveling around base and observing the other local nationals working on base. Communication was difficult. Driving on the roads (even as a passenger) was very stressful; the drivers often passed on blind curves going twice the speed limit, and they would grin or laugh when you screamed or asked them to slow down. I missed American food; Taco Bell was the first place that I ate out at when I first returned home.

After a while I started to detest the culture and people there. I would get angry, roll my eyes, and lose my patience often. I have never been a person to carry hate around in my spirit or heart, and it started to bother me that I was feeling this way. I said a prayer one day; I remember it exactly: "God, please don't let me have hate in my heart for another human being." I would be surprised by how that prayer would be answered.

I was sitting in a restaurant one day when a man approached our table with a book he had written. Wanting to be left alone, I asked him "how much?" figuring I would buy his book and he would go away. I was surprised by his answer. He told me there was no charge, he just wanted me to read the book, and asked that when someone did ask me for money that I give them even just a little bit of change to help them. He told me that he knew that we thought the people in Kosovo just went and blew the money, but it would mean a great deal to him if I would just help them even a little bit.

The man's name was Milazim Berisha, and the book titled "Escape from Kosovo" was his story about his own struggle. In that area of the world, many people have the same name; Milazim Berisha is a common name. His family was from Kosovo, but he had been sent to Switzerland to train as a pilot in hopes of a better life. When the war began in Kosovo, he came back to help his family. They had a farm from which the family had to flee. The farm would be destroyed and the house would be blown up. Even worse than losing his family home, a Serbian sniper killed his father. He talked of Albanian men being killed by decapitation and their wives being raped all in front of their children then the children having to walk over their father's dead bodies to get to the safety of the nearest refugee camps with their mother's. He talked of meeting these families at refugee camps and listening as they recounted their stories of terror and abuse.

The Serbians were killing the Albanians just because of religious reasons and territorial disputes. Even now things are not much better for the Albanians: they still have no official government, so they can't get passports, which basically traps them in Kosovo without any real hope of ever leaving.

The more I read, the more it touched my heart. I began to realize just how much these people had been through, and it broke my heart to realize that they lived the way they did because there really wasn't any choice for them. I found myself wanting to do something to help them. The land itself is beautiful, but much of it is in ruins and the people live in something even worse than what most imagine poverty to look like.

The unemployment rate is over ninety percent. I could feel the hurt and pain from the people there. I started to appreciate the fact that KBR was supporting jobs for the local nationals and I was a part of that. I had never felt so much compassion before; my heart opened up and, after reading the book, my life really has never been the same. I remember crying when I finished the book.

I was on a plane trip sitting in business class on a transatlantic flight, and all I could think about was the suffering people, the widows, orphans, homeless, and unemployed. I feel that if you don't do the best you can to help other people with the assets, compassion, and money you have currently, you will never be blessed beyond that or prosper in the future. If you cannot and will not give when you have little, God cannot trust you with greater things because you will still not give when you have more. I really do believe in getting back ten fold when you give with a pure heart.

Ever since that time, when I have been able to help people get jobs and watch their lives prosper, there is no feeling greater than that! To really feel the emotions of another person and to comprehend their gratitude and to know that you have truly made a difference in their lives, it cannot compare to money or riches. It is part of creating that ripple effect, it is an extension of what Alison's mother did for me, and it is such a beautiful thing! To not pass it on would be a shame and waste of my existence in this world.

The Albanians in Kosovo don't seem to realize that they have a hard life. They all seem to be a very happy people and they are grateful for what they have. They find a way to make the very best of a very horrible situation and never seem to be angry or resentful about the things they don't have. Don't get me wrong, I have a lot of respect and love for the Serbian people as well. I will never stereotype an entire race, religion, or culture based on negative actions of their minority groups.

After reading this book, I met a little girl that would change my life and send me on a path that I would have never imagined for myself. I was stepping out of a taxi when I noticed her: a little girl with the most beautiful blue eyes I had ever seen. She was smiling like the happiest child in the world. Somehow all the violence and hate that was going on around her failed to fade her smile or take away the joy she found in life. As soon as I got out of the taxi, she wrapped her arms around me and hugged me as if we had been old friends who hadn't seen each other in a while. I gave her some money, and from time to time I would also bring her gifts; something about this little girl touched me and I couldn't just hand her some money and walk away. I wanted to do more for her, I wanted to know more about her and about her family.

I found out that her name was Blerta, and I was able to find out where she lived, so I arranged a meeting with her family. Nobody in the family, including Blerta, spoke English, so I made arrangements to bring an interpreter with me. An Albanian co-worker/firefighter helped me out; he arranged the meeting and went with me on my first visit with Blerta's family. The family welcomed me into their home, but I was horrified by what I encountered. This wasn't a home at all! If it had been in the US, it would have been condemned; it truly should have been uninhabitable. I had passed this house many times and never thought anybody lived there because of the condition of the building. I thought it was an old abandoned building from the war. The building had no running water, no heat or air, and they used plastic jugs for a toilet. This two-room "apartment" resembled a shed more than a house.

Blerta's father had been unable to find work, and her mother worked at a local bread factory earning 100 euros per month. This family has suffered terribly, and the interpreter told me that they had lost their home during the war and were forced to live here. I noticed all of the gifts I had given Blerta were in the display case in one of the rooms. These things appeared to be the only things of value in the home. The family had also lost a set of newborn twins due to an unknown illness, and yet they were still warm and welcoming to a total stranger. Instead of feeling sorry for themselves, they accepted what they had and made do. Blerta always had her amazing smile, and I wondered how she kept that smile with all the loss she had suffered in her short life. I wondered if she ever felt sad; I hoped not.

I found myself having trouble sleeping at night knowing they were cold and often hungry; I had to do something. I decided I was going to help this family not only get a real home, but I wanted them to be able to live and eat as well. I didn't know how I was going to do this, but I was determined to find a way, so I began my quest to give Blerta and her family a home.

I began to do some research into things such as the going rates for housing and land. However, my biggest concern was the fact that they did not have a stable or official government, so I had to ensure that, if I did buy them something, they would be able to keep it in their name, have title deed, and not get run out of the place. With the help of some good people, I got the paperwork started and began to work on getting the necessary UN contracts. This process took almost a year, and work would not begin until after I left Kosovo, but Blerta and her family would eventually have a new home (see Chapter 12). I also needed money to make this happen, and although I was making good money, I knew I would need more for this, so it was time for me to move on and find a better job with better pay.

I was ready for a new adventure, and I found one waiting for me in the Middle East.

I still remember when I was a little girl, watching Abbott and Costello with the snake charmers in their Arabian-themed movies; something about those movies always made me want to visit those magical places. I remember hearing about Grace Kelly marrying a prince in some strange foreign land. Those were my fairy tales as a little girl, and I was always searching for my prince; would there be one waiting for me there?

First, I had to say goodbye to my crew. It is always difficult for me to leave people with whom I have formed a relationship, and in Kosovo everyone had to give their end-of-tour speeches in front of both shifts with all the Albanians and Serbians listening.

On my final shift before departing, I told them that they taught me more than I ever learned in the stateside fire service. I said that it was hard enough to get along with the Americans on the long 24-hour shifts in the states—yes, we would argue and bicker and have the fights that are normal with being a firefighter—but to see the Albanians and Serbians living and working together here in war-torn Kosovo, dealing with religious differences and serious issues like rape, murder, and destruction was something else.

To see these guys living in harmony most of the time and working as a team in the fire department with each other for 24 hours every other day ... it was hard to get across in words the magnitude of it all. Albanians dared not go to Serbian territory and vice versa outside of camp for fear of their lives.

To see them functioning, being productive, and bettering themselves on a daily basis in harmony and actually trusting each other with their lives on duty was absolutely amazing.

Sometimes the Albanians would actually venture off camp to weddings of the Serbian firefighters by invitation. It was rare because of the danger involved, but somehow in this firehouse they were able to forget the indifferences and become brothers and sisters.

DARE, DREAM, DISCOVER

Somehow these men and women who had been born and raised to hate and either fear or kill one another had become something different. They had become friends and family; they relied upon one another for their lives and shared meals and sleeping quarters at the end of the day. I imagine this would have been shocking to anyone outside of this small little world in which we were living, but it taught me something very important about judging others based on their country, race, or religion.

These men had discovered that being different didn't make another person bad or of less value than any other human. I often wish the rest of the world could have seen them working and living together. Maybe somehow we can all learn from these men to judge people on the quality of their hearts instead of their race or beliefs.

I lived and interacted with Muslims and Christians and was accepted and welcomed into their homes. After awhile I did not see them as Albanians and Serbians or Muslims and Christians, I saw them as family and part of the great human race that I believe was created by a loving God that wants all of His children to live together in peace and harmony. I believe that this can never happen without opening our hearts and minds. It is hard to really understand different cultures and religions by watching the news and reading books; the truth and understanding comes by looking into their eyes, hearing their stories, and walking in their shoes. If even just for one day we could all physically put ourselves in the place of other people in strange and far off lands, I know this world would be a more loving place. I learned as much from them as they learned from me in this time. I was sad to leave, but I was also excited to discover my next adventure and find out what the place of my little girl fantasies would really hold in store for me.

While I was in Kosovo, I had a bout of homesickness that led to a phone call to my dad. I had decided that when I had the chance I was going to go home and visit with him, my step-mother, and my half-brothers and sisters. For some reason I was missing my dad more than I had ever missed him in my life and I felt I needed to spend some time with him.

I called home to talk to my dad, and he told me that he was recovering from surgery; I couldn't believe what I was hearing. I remember feeling as if my entire body was going numb, my head started to spin, and I was asking what felt like a million questions. My dad explained that he had stage III colon cancer. It all began one day when he began to bleed while in the bathroom; lab tests and MRIs revealed he had a tumor that was so large that it had to be surgically removed.

To eliminate the smaller tumors he had to undergo 7-11 months of radiation and chemotherapy. He had already started his treatment, and that he hadn't told me because he didn't want me worrying when I was so far from home. He also didn't want me jumping on a plane and coming home for nothing. I would have gotten on the first plane if I had known he was having surgery, but he had convinced me as he had done with himself and everyone around him that he was going to be just fine. He told me the doctors were very hopeful and his main concern was going back to work as soon as possible.

I took a two-week break before heading to Kuwait and went to Las Vegas to spend some time with my dad and my best friend. I picked my dad up in a limousine, which was a luxury he didn't generally have in his day to day life. He worked hard for a living and earned a working man's wage, so it felt good to be able to give him some time just to relax and have fun. I took him to the Stratosphere for dinner one night, and dad just kept going on about having the best steak he had ever eaten in his life.

Dad continued to insist that his chemo and other treatments were going great and he was going to be fine in a short time. He had a strange limp, as if one leg had become shorter than the other, but dad blamed this on the diabetes that he had been diagnosed with a couple of years earlier.

We spent only three days together, but for the first time in many years we had quality time with each other. I cherish and remember those three days as one of my fondest memories with my dad.

*　　*　　*

Blerta's Smile

This is in reference to a family in Kosovo who lost their home due to the Serbian and Albanian war. I worked as a DOD contractor in Kosovo in 2002-2003. I've learned a lot from my experiences during that time.

DARE, DREAM, DISCOVER

Some people wonder why I want to help this family. They say that I should worry more about starving people in America. Well, to set the record straight, I do care about starving people in America and I do what I can to support certain charities in America. I witnessed first hand the devastating effects of the war in the Balkans.

With an 90% unemployment rate, most of the people live in poverty. I've seen countless children begging for spare change and food. At times, it would even get annoying. One day, I said a prayer for me not to be so annoyed with the uneducated and begging people in that area. I was eating dinner at a local restaurant one night when a man came by our table passing out books about the war and the suffering consequences the people faced over it. I asked him how much he wanted for the book and he replied "nothing." He said that he wanted us to remember the poor and homeless and that when they asked for money to spare some change for them.

After I read the book, my heart changed for the people of Kosovo. I read stories and saw pictures of women who had to walk across the blood of their husband's decapitated bodies with their children to flee to safety and to the nearest refugee camps. I saw the pictures of crying children. I saw the empty lifeless stares of women who lost not just their husbands, but life as they knew it.

On another occasion I was in town, upon stepping out of my taxi, I noticed a beautiful young girl with the most gorgeous blue eyes, smiling like she was the happiest little girl on earth. As soon as I got out of the taxi, she wrapped her arms around me and gave me a great big hug.

Again, my heart went out. I gave her some money and would often bring her gifts. For some reason, this girl really touched my heart. I wanted to know more about her, more about her family. Blerta was her name. I called her my Albanian Princess.

I managed to find out where she lived and arranged a meeting with her and her family with an interpreter. I wanted to do more for the family, not just give spare change. No one in the family, including Blerta, spoke English. When I first saw the house, I immediately froze. This was a house that I passed many times. I had thought for sure that no one lived in this area. The building looked worse than condemned.

The family was very friendly to me. Blerta's mother made me feel right at home. The only problem ... this really wasn't a home. There was no running water, no heat, none of the comforts of a regular home. Basically, the layout was two rooms that a family of four called home. I noticed that all of the gifts that I had given Blerta were in the family display case. It seemed to be the only items the family had of value. It was explained to me by the interpreter that the family had lost their home during the war and was forced to live in this apartment.

The father could not find a job and the mother worked at a nearby bread factory earning approximately 100 euros a month for the family to survive on. The interpreter also told me that the family had lost a set of newborn twins due to an unknown illness during the war.

I still couldn't get over Blerta's smile. She really seemed like the happiest girl on earth despite losing her home and siblings during the war. She was young *when it happened, but still, I thought; she must get cold, must get hungry, and must want her own bed. Does she ever get sad? I hope not. It's hard for me to sleep sometimes knowing that they are cold and not knowing if they have enough food.*

Maybe I can't help everyone or buy everyone a house. But when someone comes into your life and touches your heart the way they have touched mine, I feel that it was for a reason. If I can be of any assistance in making their lives a little brighter, why not? Who knows why it happened that way for me. It reminds me of something I read in the Bible before ... it says something to the effect of, when you passed by the hungry, why didn't you feed them? Why didn't you visit the sick? The imprisoned? Why didn't you help the homeless?

The Bible refers to those people as a reflection of Jesus himself. Also, the Bible talks about entertaining angels unaware. These people deserve the assistance of others just like any other human being on this Earth. We are all one creation. No one person is better or more deserving than the other.

DARE, DREAM, DISCOVER

Now don't get me wrong, I'm not trying to be some self-righteous religious person, or hypocrite who is telling anyone what they should or shouldn't do. I'm sure it's obvious I don't know the scriptures by heart ... I'm just telling my story. If anything ... I want to make sure that Blerta keeps smiling!

CHAPTER X

IRAQ
AND KUWAIT

THE AMERICAN TROOPS HAD ONLY BEEN IN IRAQ A FEW MONTHS WHEN I BEGAN MY JOURNEY THERE IN OCTOBER OF 2003, BUT BEFORE I COULD GO TO IRAQ, I HAD TO GO TO KUWAIT FOR IN-PROCESSING. I arrived in Kuwait during Ramadan. Ramadan occurs during the ninth month of the Muslim lunar calendar and is considered the holiest month of the year for Muslims.

Ramadan is observed by Muslims all over the world as they take this time to reflect on family, community, and their spirituality; part of this involves fasting during the day and eating very light evening meals. The exact date that Ramadan begins changes each year with the calendar and given that it is actually based on the moon, the actual date is never known until the night before. When it begins in a Muslim country there is no doubt that this is a very holy time that is observed.

At the time, I didn't understand the culture or the point of not being able to chew gum or drink water during the day and it seemed crazy to me that I could be thrown in jail for violating these things, but I am also a firm believer in respecting the culture of the people, no matter where I am, so I did my best to observe their traditions and be respectful of their faith. Kuwait seemed much more modern than I had imagined. I was shocked to find they had Starbucks and Burger King along with many other places familiar to me. I so badly wanted to explore this new place that I found myself in, but we were not allowed to go anywhere. We were watched and protected by KBR security during our time there, and often these men reminded me of rent-a-cops in the US: they tried to act big and bad and were always going on about how they had thwarted some kind of bomb plot or something just as far fetched. The fire and police departments have always had a bit of a friendly rivalry going on between them, but this was just ridiculous.

The egos of these security teams were huge; one would have thought they were the Secret Service by the way they went on and on about their own heroics. They also had a good deal of power over the rest of us, and the security teams took full advantage of this by implementing rules that made little to no sense at all, from threatening to fire us to basically keeping all of us prisoner because we couldn't go anywhere without them. We were herded like cattle to go from one place to another while the security teams behaved like drill sergeants in the military. I found the entire experience laughable, but I was glad to get out of Kuwait and head for Iraq. I was given the choice to wait up to one month for a military charter flight to Iraq or go on a three-day convoy.

Being the person I am and having the need for some true adventure mixed in with a little danger, I opted for the three-day convoy. I was anxious to get there and I couldn't take the watchdog security force anymore. Finally I was headed for Iraq and Camp Speicher.

Camp Speicher is located near Tikrit, Iraq and is named in honor of Captain Michael Scott Speicher, the only MIA from Operation Desert Storm. Then Navy Lieutenant Commander Michael Scott Speicher, who would later be promoted to Captain, was shot down in his F-18 on January 17, 1991 and originally presumed dead. While there were several claims that Captain Speicher had been either killed or devoured by animals, none of these claims offered much in real evidence, and the Navy would list him as captured in October of 2002.

DARE, DREAM, DISCOVER

Camp Speicher is the former Al Sahra Iraqi Air Force Base and is large at 25 square miles. The barracks where soldiers are living once housed the students of the Iraqi Air Force Academy. Camp Speicher serves as a support hub for soldiers based north of Baghdad. The camp has a hospital and serves as a storage depot for fuel and supplies. It also is a major center for repairs to trucks and tanks. Most recently it was headquarters to the 101st Airborne Division.

During my trip into Iraq I found that I was a little scared at times, though it was nothing that I couldn't handle; we had to stop for a few IEDs (improvised explosive devices) in the roads on the way up. We had to wait for the bomb squad to defuse the bombs and clear the road before we could move, so we had to wait for as long as two hours. Until we received the all-clear signal, we were sitting ducks, bull's eye targets on the road.

It seemed like in every town we drove through, bare foot children would come running through the desert looking for us to throw them food, candy, or toys. I guess they started to know the convoy routes and times. They were so cute and I really wanted to help them, but at the same time I was very cautious, as these women and children were considered a threat to our lives. There were many stories of women suicide bombers and innocent looking people blowing up and killing our troops on a daily basis.

I remember one radio report on the drive up: A Chinook aircraft carrying over 40 people that were going home after their tour in Iraq was shot out of the sky in the Baghdad area. Again, similar to the emotions that I carried around from 9/11, I now felt a greater sense of loss for the people who were risking their lives for the fight against terrorism.

I was so happy to finally make it to Camp Speicher safe and sound. Finally I could begin to get myself settled in and get to work.

Arriving in Iraq I found myself both physically and emotionally exhausted; we arrived no worse for wear, but we had to be alert every minute of the journey. At any time we could have come across an IED or taken fire from insurgents. Camp Speicher was in Tikrit, Saddam Hussein's hometown, and soon there would be a great deal of excitement and media attention focused on this town in northern Iraq.

DARE, DREAM, DISCOVER

I was surprised by the weather in northern Iraq. The media always spoke of the very hot summers, when the temperature in many parts of Iraq could climb as high as 140°F, but they never mentioned the winters in the northern regions.

The wind was bitter cold and felt like it could cut through you like a knife, and in the desert when the wind blew, so did the sand. Everything in Iraq is covered in sand and dust. Blowing sand is not only painful when it hits bare skin, but it can also cut into the skin and scratch the eyes. Often, even if the day is hot, the nights can be bitter cold. It is not uncommon for the temperature to drop as much as 40 degrees within a couple of hours. On occasion it can snow in northern Iraq, but it is more likely to rain. Growing up in Florida I had seen some pretty heavy rains, but I wasn't prepared to see it in a country that is mostly desert.

I soon discovered that when it rained outside, it would also rain inside of my work trailer. It was a challenge to keep myself and my work dry and still get everything done on time. To keep from getting covered in mud going from one place to another on base, I would have to wear rubber boots that went up to my knees.

These boots were heavy and often tough to walk in, but they were certainly better than sinking into the mud, and that mud could be hiding anything from bugs to snakes underneath the surface.

I believe many civilian contractors for the Department of Defense sign up because they honestly believe they can do something to make a difference and help the troops; I certainly did. However, I was as shocked by the attitude of some of the contract workers that were there with me as much as I was by the conditions.

While most people do not take on a job simply for satisfaction, and most did sign up because the money would help them and their families, I was not pleased with the attitude of many toward the troops. It seemed to me that many found the troops a nuisance. That made me mad because I knew that, without those troops, we would have no reason to have the jobs we had.

I would often find myself crying because of the conditions the troops had to live in. They didn't have a decent PX where they could get snacks or even some of the more basic day-to-day living items, and, contrary to popular opinion, the military supplies very little of their basic needs, including razors. There wasn't a decent laundry service, and yet they were expected to have their uniforms clean and in order, which had to be difficult. It also appeared that many didn't even have uniforms that matched; the tops and bottoms would be different in some way or another. I would see clothing hanging outside on makeshift clothes lines on a regular basis, which more often than not had to be cleaned in cold water because hot water was not always available to them.

They did have decent meals most of the time, but I was troubled by all of the basic necessities they were lacking. It bothered me that these men and women were putting their lives on the line–many were dying outside of the wire–and I was working for one of the biggest contracting firms providing them with basic life support, but we weren't even providing them with clean clothes and hot water.

I'll never forget December 13, 2003, the day Saddam Hussein was captured. I could not believe he was right there in Tikrit and had probably been there most of the time. That day was the happiest I had ever seen the soldiers since my arrival. Their unit, the 2nd Infantry Division, had been involved in his capture and they were thrilled. Saddam would never torture another innocent person again, and maybe in time what our troops had done might make it so the Iraqi people could live in a place that was both safe and peaceful. I don't know if they realized at that time that they had become a piece of world history, they were just happy that they had captured a man that had terrorized a country for too many years.

Bombs were going off on a regular basis. Many of them had been part of Saddam's arsenal and the US military was getting rid of them in the only way they could, by setting them off, but it was still disturbing to see the mushrooms clouds cover the sky when they did this. In addition, the security situation was growing worse. Things were heating up between the troops and the insurgents; more troops and contractors were being killed when they went outside of the wire.

As time went by, I got to the point that I didn't notice the bombs so much and would even sleep through many of them. I could deal with the living conditions and the bombs, but I was becoming more and more frustrated with the inability to do the job that I thought I had been sent to do. Everything seemed to be back-logged, including living containers (little metal-framed shed-type buildings) for the soldiers. I hated looking around that post everyday and seeing what wasn't being done and finding myself in a position that rendered me helpless to make any of it happen.

When I was offered a position with a small company in Kuwait with basically the same job, but with the ability to get the supplies that were needed to the troops in a reasonable amount of time, I jumped at the chance. I wanted to make a difference, and there was no way I was going to be able to do that with the company I was with at the time. After spending almost seven months in Iraq, I was headed back to Kuwait to a new job and the hopes of finally doing something to make life at least a little bit better for the troops.

My job in Kuwait proved to be exactly what I needed. I was able to get supplies to the troops, usually within 15 to 20 days from the time they were ordered. With several bases in Kuwait and the ability to procure most items right there, a great deal of the red tape that often held up shipments was reduced. Once we had procured the items from an order request, we put them on a truck and sent them to one of the bases in Kuwait and had the items there within one or two days.

This was when I began to learn about the Muslim culture and people, and as time went by I came to appreciate what they do for our troops. Unlike the contractors that I worked with in Iraq, the Muslim people genuinely cared about the troops and wanted them to have the things they needed. They did more than just show up and do the minimum to get paid; their actions showed me every day how much it mattered to them that the troops had the vital supplies and life support services they needed. For a people who don't work the same working hours as most of the Western world, they certainly were more than willing to work harder and longer than I expected.

There were more days than I can count that our team would put in 12 to 15 hours and turn around the next day to do it all over again. The people I worked with never complained and never acted as if they were put out by these long hard hours. During Ramadan the Muslim people don't usually put in too many hours at work because they are fasting and tire easily, yet they showed up every single day for work and, instead of resting as most do during this time, they continued to put in long hours to ensure that the troops had what they needed without having to wait any longer than necessary. I have heard people say that the Muslims are lazy because they don't work the kind of hours that most countries do; what I discovered was that they are anything but lazy and, when needed, they will work as much as needed to get the job done and do it well. They are not used to the kind of hours that most of us put in and due to their religious observations it is often difficult for them to put in an eight hour day, but when it matters they are more willing than anyone I have ever worked with to give all they have and then some to make sure that the job is done.

Like most Americans, I had heard the horror stories about Muslims and how they hate American's and Christians. I am both American and Christian, and all I have ever felt from the Muslim people is love.

Several months after I began working in Kuwait, my father began to lose his battle with cancer. Despite his refusal to give in to the sickness and despite his insistence to me that he was going to be just fine and was getting better everyday, the cancer finally began to take hold of his body. I decided to go home for a visit and spend some time with my dad. As always, he did all he could to hide just how sick he was from me, but I knew he wasn't well. The company that I worked for during this time knew my dad was sick, and they had not only helped me get home to the states to spend this time with him, but they also sent flowers to my dad's home. I remember my dad smiling and saying how nice this was of them. It meant so much to him that people cared, and I believe it made him feel better knowing that I worked with people that cared about me.

During this visit I also spent some time with my younger sister Nickie. She had gone through cosmetology school and was working her butt off to just scrape by. As we sat there talking one evening, she told me how it didn't matter how good she was, it was going to take her at least five years to really even begin making any kind of decent money. She seemed frustrated by this because it didn't seem to matter how hard she worked, she would be stuck just getting by for a long time.

I suggested that she come to Kuwait and work with me for awhile; if nothing else I was making enough at this time that I could give her a living allowance and have her take care of my hair. It didn't take long before Nickie was working with me and making her own way in Kuwait. I was happy to have her with me, but we were both torn about not being home with our father.

We had struggled with the decision to go back or wait for a few weeks. It was so very expensive to make the trip back to the States and there was work to be done. We finally realized that if we didn't go home soon we might never have the chance again, so Nickie got on a plane and I planned to follow her in a couple of days after I finished up some work. It seemed as if I had barely dropped my sister off at the airport when the phone rang. It was Sue, my stepmother, and she said that if I had anything that I wanted to say to my dad I had best do it then because he wasn't going to make it much longer.

As Sue held the phone to my dad's ear, I told him to just hang on, that Nickie was already on her way and I would be there soon. I told him how much I loved him and just talked to him for awhile. I knew in my heart this would be the last time I ever had that chance and I tried to express everything that I felt for him and to let him know how much he meant to me.

Although he wasn't able to speak, I believe that he heard me. My dad would pass just a short time after this.

IRAQ AND KUWAIT

He wasn't able to hold on until Nickie got there, but he knew she was on her way home and I know that brought him peace. Nickie got off the plane to see her mother and our brother there and she knew instantly that dad was gone. There was no way that Sue would have left him at that time if he hadn't passed. Nickie still feels bad because she didn't get to say the things that she wanted to say to him while he was alive, but I have no doubt that he already knew what was in her heart.

My bosses once again came through for me; they put me on a plane and sent me home immediately to be with my family and say goodbye to my dad. I couldn't believe the outpouring of love and support from everyone I worked with before I left and after I came back. I was met with hugs and compassion from everyone. I had lost the person that I loved most in this world and my heart was breaking, but I also knew how lucky I was to be surrounded by these kind and loving people who never once let me forget that they cared about me.

As painful as the loss of my dad has been for me, it also gave me a different perspective of the Muslim people and what they are really like. Sadly the media seldom portray them as anything but a terrorist group who hate Americans, but the people I met were nothing like that at all. The people I met offered kindness, compassion, and love to two Christian American women who had lost their father. At that time there wasn't a culture, religious, or race difference between us, but instead there was love and kindness when I needed it more than I ever had in my life.

*   *   *

My Hero Forever,
Dad,

You will never be forgotten by me. I'm so proud of you for what you did in your lifetime. You joined the Air Force and fought in Vietnam. You gave me life. You loved me. Even though I was raised with my mother ... you are the one I give all the credit and honor to. I love you and I thank you.

You dedicated your life to helping other kids by coaching Little League Softball.

You were a strong advocate in incorporating women into the league ... you always gave me strength, the push and drive that I needed to succeed in life.

I will never forget the times that we did share together. I will never forget how much I missed you and would look at your picture when we were not together. I will never forget laughing with you, singing with you, and smiling at you. I loved your blue eyes and bright smile.

I admire your strength in fighting cancer. You never wanted anyone to see your sadness and pain.

Thank you for letting me know before you passed away that your life was fulfilled in knowing that your kids "turned out to be great."

I love you now and forever ... even though you are not with me physically ... your memory will live forever in my heart and soul. I miss you so much, just like I did when I was a little girl.

CHAPTER XI

MY PRINCE
CHARMING

I HAD FOUND A PLACE WHERE I FELT LIKE I BELONGED AND WHERE I WAS MAKING A DIFFERENCE FOR THE TROOPS AND ALSO FOR THE PEOPLE THAT WERE WORKING WITH ME. I loved my job, I loved that I was making very good money and that I could see making even more in the very near future. The only thing missing in my life was love.

I would happen to have a chance meeting with the possible Prince Charming of my dreams with a little help from a friend. My friend had mentioned "BT" to me a few times and he thought that we might find a way to do business with one another. BT was well known for his business and support work for the US government, and I believed that if I could get his company to work with the company that I was working for, we could offer so much more to the troops and make both companies more successful in the process.

My friend insisted that I meet with BT as soon as possible, and while I expected to do business with him,

MY PRINCE CHARMING

I never expected that I would fall head over heels in love with him. I remember taking extra care when I was getting ready to go to my first meeting with BT. I spent hours spiral-curling my hair and picking out just the right clothes. I finally decided on a black Tommy Hilfiger shirt dress with a pair of black pants and black shoes to go with it. I wanted to look just right; I wanted new business and new contracts and I wanted it badly.

From the moment I walked into his office and laid eyes on BT (he was also dressed in black), I was infatuated with him from the start. He was one of the most handsome men I had ever seen in my life. He had an air of confidence to him that only very powerful, very attractive men have.

I began talking about Iraq, my experiences there, and ideas that I had on business development. I really wanted to do business with him, but more than that I also realized I was very attracted to this man. I tried to avoid letting that get in my way, but as I was talking to him about Iraq and work, he began talking about Dubai, hookers, and parties. He had a flat screen television in his office, and at one point he turned the volume up. Imagine my surprise to hear my favorite song at the time, Naughty

Girl by Beyonce. BT told me he was throwing a party the next night at his place and asked if I would like to come. Was he kidding? Of course I wanted to go! I was eager to experience this side of Kuwait. I was so excited that, the next day, I spent most of my time thinking about what we would talk about at the party. One side of me thought this night could be the turning point to really get business to take off, but I couldn't help but think about the very sexy man with whom I might be doing business with; he would certainly be an added bonus.

There were definitely sparks flying between us at the party, but I was still more interested in business than I was in this man. I got the feeling that BT was rather full of himself, and he seemed like the type who liked having his ego stroked often. I sure wasn't going to be stroking anyone's ego, no matter how good-looking or powerful they were. Chasing after men and stroking egos is not my style. I feel that if someone really wants to be with me, they will. I don't want to ever talk anyone into being with me or proving myself worthy; I did that enough in the past in business and in past relationships. I made a vow never to do that again.

MY PRINCE CHARMING

After the party, I sent BT an e-mail explaining that I was looking forward to a long-lasting business relationship with him and his company.

I figured I had made my point very clear at that time, that all I wanted from him was a business relationship, but when he responded to my e-mail with a very simple "Yeah in Dubai," I laughed it off. I remember thinking to myself that was not something that would every really happen. I doubted he even meant it.

Later my friend would tell me that BT had said that he needed to convince me to join his company. I couldn't believe it. He wanted me to join his company? Did he really expect me to just up and quit the job I had? I had responsibilities, I certainly wasn't going to just toss that out the window and go running because he wanted me to do so. But for many reasons, some even beyond my own explanation, I kept finding myself getting closer and closer to BT's office.

BT had mentioned to me that on Fridays they all sat around the office having drinks, so one Friday I worked up the nerve and went over there. I arrived with only the intention of having a couple of drinks and leaving, but it seems destiny had another plan for me that day. A couple of drinks turned into many drinks. BT was pouring the drinks and I kept accepting them. The party started in his office and ended up in the bathroom where he had followed me. It was right there in the bathroom where he kissed me for the first time. Many events of that night are fuzzy, but that kiss will forever be burned in my memory. I had been kissed before, but I had never been kissed like that! When someone talks about a kiss that makes you weak in the knees, I now understand exactly what they are talking about.

After leaving the office, BT invited me to a party. He said the party was being held by some of his Kuwaiti friends; what he didn't mention is that they were Kuwaiti royalty. There at this party were some of the most beautiful women I have ever seen. They were not in the traditional abayah that women in that part of the world normally wear–instead they had on shorter black outfits–and they were dancing all over the room. This was a private club complete with a DJ that was playing great music. It was beautifully decorated in the Arabic style with pillows all over the place, and they even had private rooms. At some point during that night, I found myself in one of those rooms with BT. We didn't make love that night, but things certainly became much more heated than just the kiss in his office earlier. I'll never forget what he said to me in that room. He looked me straight in the eyes–I swear he didn't even blink–and told me "You are mine now and you don't even know what that means."

He ran his fingers through my hair and told me I looked like a princess, and at that moment I felt like one. I can still see his eyes staring at me. They were dark and very intense; they reminded me of a predator watching its prey, but at the same time he was falling in love with his prey. I would have probably run as fast and as far as I could had I realized at that moment how many had been this man's prey, but I was also convinced that I would not be like that. I was smarter and stronger than that, there was no way I would allow myself to fall into his trap.

The following days my head was filled with thoughts of BT. I wanted to hear his voice, I wanted to talk to him, to be near him, I wanted to know more about him, and I wanted him. He invited me to various places with him; sometimes we would go to parties, other times we would go to one of his homes. It seemed like nobody really lived there, but rather were just used on occasion. I wondered how many houses he owned, as there always seemed to be more, and I also wondered how many women he took to these places.

The more time I spent with this man, the harder I fell for him. He was certainly a playboy to say the least, but he was also one of the most decent and caring people I have ever known. He helped so many people with his company, from his employees to the troops. He brought in many people from places such as India and Pakistan that had no way of making a living in their home countries and gave them jobs; not just any job, but a job that would help them take care of their families and have a good chance at a decent life. He seemed to take genuine pleasure in helping others and watching them flourish. I was awed by his kindness and generosity towards others and I was thrilled to be spending time with him.

It didn't take long before things started to get serious between us. One night when BT was at my house, he asked me "What would it take to make you only mine?" Being sarcastic, I told him a big fat diamond ring. He seemed surprised. "Is that all?" he asked me.

"That and spending as much time as you can with me," I told him. I honestly didn't think he was sober enough to remember any of it the next day. After that he was constantly trying to get me to go to Dubai with him, and I kept telling him that I couldn't. I had work or I was working on a big deal; it was always work that kept me from going, and he seemed impressed by my dedication to my work, but he really wanted me to go to Dubai with him. Finally he came up with an idea that would work: I could fly out to Dubai one night after work and, since it was only about an hour flight, I could come back on a flight very early the next morning. I was so excited about going to Dubai; BT had talked about it so much that I almost felt like I had already been there.

Arriving in Dubai was like something out of the movie Pretty Woman. We were picked up at the airport in a Mercedes Benz, and although I didn't think anything was wrong with our ride, BT complained to the driver because there wasn't water and a cold hand towel for him in the car. Sitting there all starry-eyed, I looked at BT and said, "I like being your baby." He looked at me and smiled when he told me, "You don't even know." I had no idea what that meant, but I really wasn't worried about it; I felt like I was walking through one of the fairytales that

I dreamed of from my childhood. As we pulled up to the hotel, I was awestruck. There were colored lights coming from every angle of the hotel, and in some ways it was like an adult version of Cinderella's castle. I couldn't believe I was going to be staying there, and making it feel even more like a fantasy, everyone was falling over themselves to make sure we were happy. I felt like royalty, and the night hadn't even started yet.

We were escorted to the business center, and on the way BT met up with two gentlemen who seemed to know him rather well. BT signaled for me to join them on the elevator and we headed for our room.

I remember wondering who these men were and why they had bags in their hands. I couldn't even begin to imagine what they might have in them, and I really didn't give it too much thought until we reached our room and they opened the bags.

We didn't stay in just any room; we were in the royal suite. It was beyond my wildest imagination. Everything seemed bigger than life; the suite was larger than many homes I have seen in my lifetime. My head was spinning from everything that was happening. Then the two men who had come with us opened their bags. They started pulling out jewelry boxes and opening them. And not just any jewelry, but diamonds–big fat diamonds; there were rings, earrings and necklaces. I couldn't believe my eyes, and I was still a bit confused. It hadn't occurred to me that these men were here for me.

When BT told me to "pick one" I almost fell over. Did he just tell me to pick one of those amazing diamonds? I had to be dreaming; there was no way on earth this could possibly be real.

BT reminded me that I had told him that all he had to do was get me a big rock and there they were; now all I had to do was pick one. My head was really spinning. I wasn't sure if I was going to pass out or burst into tears, but somehow I managed to hold it together and started trying on rings. At one point I had on three rings at once. I finally decided on a square cut diamond with several other diamonds around it; it was big enough to practically cover my entire finger. After I picked the ring, BT asked me if I wanted anything else, and I told him "no."

He then asked me to pick out a few other pieces. I didn't ask for whom and, honestly, I didn't want to know. I knew there were other women, but if I didn't think about them, then I didn't have to deal with the reality that I might have been only his now, but he was not only mine. I was happy at that moment and I wasn't going to let thoughts of others ruin that moment for me.

I told BT that night that he had made me the happiest girl in the world. He made a sarcastic remark about how that would fade in time because that is what they all had said in the past.

BT had a friend coming over and we all went out to a club that night. We almost got thrown out because I was dancing rather erotically against BT, and that is not allowed in Dubai. I guess the bouncer thought I was a prostitute because of the way we were dancing. BT laughed and said something to him about me being his wife or girlfriend – I am not sure exactly what was said – and we were told not to do that anymore.

While Dubai is pretty liberal, they still have rules, and I didn't know it was forbidden. Not only did I have the time of my life that night, but my life was about to take a huge U-turn. Soon I would be living in the lap of luxury with more than I could have ever conjured up in my fantasies.

MY PRINCE CHARMING

As I look back at that night, I realize that, in many ways, it was similar to Pretty Woman. I have never been a prostitute, but I was as wide-eyed and more naïve than Julia Roberts' character and, unlike in the movie, I didn't have to give the diamonds back. From time to time I think about that night and wonder if Julia Roberts' character really got her happy ending or if they just faded to black before reality set in.

CHAPTER XII

GROWING PAINS

OVER THE NEXT SEVERAL WEEKS I FOUND MYSELF
MOVING CLOSER AND CLOSER TO WORKING FOR BT.
The company I was currently working for was beginning
to give me trouble and I was having difficulty getting
paid. I was also starting to question their business ethics.
I had collected over $20 million in back payments from
other contracts for them, but they weren't even paying my
salary as promised. I loved my job, but I certainly wasn't
putting in 15-hour days for nothing. When I finally had
enough of the empty promises and feeling uncomfortable
with the business practices, I realized it was time to move
on.

BT had made it clear that he wanted me to work with
his company, and I liked everything I had heard about his
company and his business ethics, so I finally gave in and
went to work for him.

If I hadn't already fallen in love with BT, I would
have at least ended up smitten when I went to work with
him. He challenged me every single day to do better and

encouraged me to push myself beyond what I believed I could do. It had been a long time since someone believed in me the way he did. Alison's mom had believed in me, as did Mr. Harris, but in many ways they were different than BT. I always wanted to do well to show them that they were right to believe in me, but with BT it was more than that. I wanted so much for him to be proud of me, but I also wanted to do well for myself. He not only believed in me, he helped me learn to believe in myself.

I loved what I was doing, and BT made me feel as if I could do anything I set my mind to. I also felt as if I challenged this brilliant man with my work ethic and drive, as he seemed to be competing with me on some level. If I came in an hour early to work, he would stay three hours later at the end of the day. I almost felt as if we were competing to see who could go the longest on any given work day. I generally lost this competition–he was able to go and go until I was ready to drop–but I loved the challenge and I always felt as if he was proud of me for putting in as much as I did.

My job was to get government service contracts, so I set myself a goal to sell port-a-johns. The port-a-johns that most military base camps had were terrible; they were like the basic port-a-john on a construction site: hard plastic, no running water, and in the desert heat they would start to stink very quickly.

Living on the base camps is never easy on the troops, but I believe that small things can make life a little more bearable for them. Being away from home and family for a long stretch of time is tough on them, so if I could make their lives just a little bit better by offering port-a-johns that had porcelain bowls and running water, I hoped that in some way they would feel less isolated from the rest of the world.

I accomplished my goal by getting a contract to sell 80 of our port-a-johns to Camp Virginia in Kuwait. This contract brought in over a million dollars, and I continued to push to supply other camps as well. By the time I had finished this project, I had sold 300 port-a-johns, as well as one year service contracts to go with them, to several camps in both Kuwait and Iraq. This was a good deal for both our company and the government because they owned them outright instead of leasing them as they did with the plastic ones. Even with a service contract, the government was saving money and we kept people working to maintain them.

GROWING PAINS

I had many different job titles. I was in charge of business development; one might also call me a project manager. I was responsible for all requirements getting met in the contracts that I secured from beginning to end. It was up to me to go out and get the contract, and then I had to make sure that the orders were filled and delivered on time, as well as making sure that everyone that worked for the company on the base camps had everything in order.

This ranged from their paperwork to having the appropriate badges for the camp they would be working on. Whatever needed to be done, I did it, and I loved every minute of it. I was good at what I did and I knew it; I was also sure BT knew this as well.

While my job was everything I could imagine, I still wasn't happy. BT is a great businessman and a good person. He has made life better for so many through his business by working to give the troops the things they needed, and by going through the long process to hire workers who really needed the job to take care of themselves and provide for their families. He is one of the greatest men anyone could know ... as long as he isn't their boyfriend. I had been lavished with amazing gifts–I had clothes and jewelry, and even a Hummer H2 (which made me feel safer on the roads there because the way people drive in Kuwait is the most insane thing I have ever seen) – but what I didn't have was the man that I had fallen head over heels in love with. His comment from the night he gave me the diamond ring would often ring true in my ears as I would sit at home alone while he was off doing things that I could only imagine. I knew there were other women, and I was beginning to realize that no matter how many times he told me how special I was or how much he loved me, needed me, or wanted me, that he would never be with just me.

At one point I even said something to BT about having all of the finest things in life but sitting at home alone dying of a broken heart. To anyone who might pass by and look at the life I had, they would have thought I had everything. I didn't want for anything, I didn't look at price tags when buying things, and my friend Alison laughs when she talks about how I have been known to convert entire rooms into closets, but I was missing the one thing in life that I had always been searching for: love. I wanted love, but the man that I loved seldom had the time for me, and I knew that wasn't going to change. My biggest accomplishments in Kuwait occurred after meeting BT. One of these accomplishments was bringing my sister Nickie over and helping her find a job. Eventually, she would come to work with us.

BT told me that it made no difference to him that she was my sister; she would have to pull her own weight and keep up with the rest of us if she wanted to keep her job. BT helped me bring her to Kuwait and he gave her a chance. I suspect he did that because he knew it would make me happy to have my sister with me, and he was right about that. It was good to have someone close to me there and I knew I could trust her.

As Nickie began to learn the business, she was able to take up some of the slack so we could get twice as much work done and cover more area. I was so proud of her; she took on the job and she did it well. Not only did I have my sister with me, but I had helped her find a way to make a good living so she could take care of herself without having to worry about not having enough money to pay her bills.

To this day I feel my greatest accomplishment was

getting a home for Blerta and her family in Kosovo. I had changed jobs and come to Kuwait so I could make enough money to make this dream of mine a reality. Getting a home for them was no small task, and without the help of BT and a special Major in the US Army, I don't know if I would have ever been able to cut through all of the red tape myself.

We were able to find them a proper apartment (there are very few single-residence dwellings in Kosovo) with all of the furnishings, including a couch, beds, dining room table, silverware, pots and pans, linen, decorations, washer and dryer, and stove. I will never forget the day I gave Blerta's father the cash for all of these things. I remember how I felt that day as I counted the money and was able to place it in his hands with his wife and children beside him.

Tears of joy came to his eyes. The tears and the look on his face said it all, but he also kept thanking me. I could never take credit for all of it, because everything was about team work and support in getting this done. The US Army Major did so much coordinating with the UN, and his contacts and knowledge made this process easier than it would have been without his help.

I still don't know what I would have done had I not met the Major when I was trying to sell the port-a-johns to the various military posts. He told me when I first approached him that my looks would only get me so far. He was interested in doing business with our company, but if I thought that being pretty was going to ensure his business, I was wrong.

I had better prove to him that our company could handle the job or he would bounce me out of there so fast I wouldn't know what happened. I guess I proved myself to him because, when it came to getting Blerta her home, he was one of my greatest champions. Many times he managed to cut through some of the red tape that nobody else could get through.

We wanted to ensure that everything was 110% legal because, due to the political climate in Kosovo, often it is all too easy for someone to lose their home without compensation or any assistance in finding another place to live. We wanted to be covered beyond a shadow of any doubt that no one would be able to take away their property. We were able to accomplish all of these things and give this family something they had never known; a secure place to live.

BT had been incredibly instrumental in helping me achieve this dream. He always knew I could do it, even on the days when I felt like I was running into brick wall after brick wall. He helped me in every way possible. He believed in me and my dream, and when it was all said and done, he had a made my dreams come true again. But for all of the dreams he made come true, I wasn't happy, because it was becoming very clear that the one dream I really wanted would never come true. He would never be mine; not completely.

I had attended a conference that had some brochures about the Dominican Republic, and I started thinking about moving there. In fact, I was so taken with it that I actually purchased property to build a house there without ever even visiting the country. I began to make plans to move on and go to the Dominican Republic.

I informed BT of my plans, and he came up with an alternative idea for me. It took me quite some time to finally agree with his suggestion, but as he always did, he finally wore me down and I agreed to accept his offer and make a move to Dubai. My life was about to take another

GROWING PAINS

huge turn, and I had no idea that I was about to jump into a new phase of my life that would take me on a road that I could not even imagine. Before I could move on to the next phase of my life, however, I had one last project that I needed to complete. So, before I could head to Dubai, I packed my things and headed out for a new adventure in Pakistan.

*   *   *

I had experienced so much in Kuwait; I was a little sad to leave. I had learned about the people that most only hear about on the news. I was pleasantly surprised to see what a loving and compassionate people the Kuwaiti people really are. Like most Americans, I had heard negative things about Muslims on the news and from other Americans. Even to this day, I find myself trying to explain that Muslims are not our enemy and that the Muslim religion does not teach hate. Like any walk of life, every race, creed, and religion has good and bad people. Not all Muslims are like Osama bin Laden; in fact, most are not. They teach and practice love and kindness for everyone.

These people opened their hearts and their homes to both me and my sister. They were there for us when our father passed, and they fussed at me for working too much. They bent over backwards to help the American troops, not just because there was money involved, but also because they love the Americans. The Americans helped the Kuwaitis during Desert Storm.

When Iraq invaded the small nation of Kuwait on August 2, 1990, the American troops wasted no time, getting into Kuwait only five days later. They were joined by 30 other nations committed to defending, protecting, and freeing the Kuwaiti people. It would take several months to restore stability and peace in Kuwait, but the Americans and their allies did their job and gave the Kuwaitis their home back.

The people of Kuwait have always been more than grateful for the assistance of the troops, and they do all that they can to show their gratitude; sadly they are often met with bias and even hate based solely on their faith. To these people the Americans are their heroes–saviors in a way. I have yet to meet a single Kuwaiti who would not give the food off of their table or the clothes off of their back to help an American. They genuinely love them and appreciate what was done for them, but the media doesn't report about things like that; I guess it doesn't make for good headlines. I wish that every American had the chance to spend a year in Kuwait and spend time with the people there because I believe they would come back with a very different view of the Muslims as a whole. These are very good people who now have American military bases in their country; they work in them, support them, and are grateful to have them. Sadly, most Americans just don't see any of this.

I was also very surprised to see how the women in Kuwait are treated. The news carries stories of abused Muslim women who are treated with little respect and seen as less than dogs. Let me tell you that this is not true in Kuwait. The women are loved, adored, and downright spoiled. These women work outside of the home if they wish, their husbands revere them, and they are treated as someone very precious by the men in Kuwait.

Once again, all Muslims are stereotyped due to a few countries that have their own way of doing things. From my experience in Kuwait, women are highly regarded and often treated better than most women I have met anywhere else in the world.

DARE, DREAM, DISCOVER

My greatest hope as I tell you my story is that you will at least be open-minded about any culture, any race, any gender, any human being. We share this earth, but sadly we seldom share it in peace because one group hates another for reasons that are seldom clear or rational. Until we learn to accept and even celebrate our differences, we will never know peace.

*   *   *

This blog entry was made after dealing with people on blog sites that expressed hate towards Muslims. They acted as if hating them made them more American or more patriotic. I wrote this in hopes of getting through to some that their hate really didn't make any sense:

Well, I have mentioned to some of you that, in addition to the real estate business; I am also a consultant in support of US contracts in Iraq, Kuwait and Pakistan. I have been supporting US government contracts since 2003.

Regardless of my opinion of the war and if we should or should not be there, we are there and I

GROWING PAINS

play a big part in supporting the US soldiers, as well as Iraqis and other TCNs (third country nationals).

Some of what my job involves is ensuring that deliveries of life-support equipment and supplies get to various camps throughout Iraq, but I also create local jobs for Iraqis, Indians, Pakistanis, and Egyptians. The majority of the delivery drivers are TCNs, the same as with the work force that supports construction projects and services that we perform on the US base camps. I would say that only 20% of civilian support is done by US citizens; the rest are people from other countries. I'm talking about civilians for contract support, not soldiers.

I get confused by people who make comments on being in support of the war, but make strong statements against the Iraqi people and against their religion. Yes, the terrorists are bad, and we are not there to help them; we are there to help rebuild Iraq, and that involves helping Muslims. Whether you agree with the Muslim religion or not, we are helping them. By assisting them to establish a stable government, they will be able to prosecute through their judicial system the terrorists and bad guys.

Also, we are helping them build the prisons that will detain the terrorists. Yes, we ... American citizens. Yes, your tax dollars are going towards construction of Iraqi prisons, Iraqi hospitals, Iraqi schools, and Iraqi police training facilities, just to name a few, not to mention what we are doing in Afghanistan.

Did anyone tune in to General Petraeus's briefings on rebuilding Iraq? Because what he discussed are some of the things that are happening already. From what I hear from some people, it seems to me that there many people are unclear about what we are really doing there.

Whether you agree or disagree that we went in based on the threat of weapons of mass destruction, whether you agree or disagree that we are taking a stance and fighting against terrorism, how can you not see that we are helping the very people that most people are against in the states: Muslims.

I say "most people" in the states hoping that I'm wrong, because I have been around thousands of Muslims and I do not care if everyone on this site blacklists me because of my belief that all Muslims are not bad. I worked in an office in Kuwait in which

GROWING PAINS

99% of the staff were Muslims, and they worked directly for a DOD contract company that supported over 300 million dollars worth of supplies to our US troops. I watched these people put their heart and soul into moving these supplies forward, which meant working 12-15 hours a day, 7 days a week. Yes, I worked with them and I got to know them and their families really well in the two years that I spent there.

Also, I get irked when people think that I am not patriotic ... I spent 11 years at Eglin Air Force Base. I currently travel into Iraq quite frequently. I honor and respect my home country and our US troops. I also respect the Muslim people that are not extremist. I will never fit into the box of supporting our US troops and the war but having to hate Muslims. OMG! Am I the only one here who feels this way? It sure seems like it. But that is O.K. I've gone against the grain my entire life; I'm used to it. Good grief, I could write a book here. Hmmmmm ... that is a good thought.

CHAPTER XIII

PAKISTAN

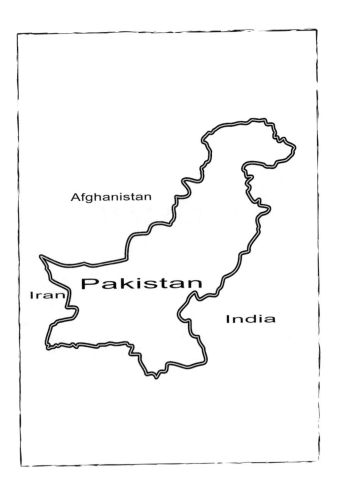

ON OCTOBER 8, 2005, AN EARTHQUAKE THAT REGISTERED 7.6 ON THE RICHTER SCALE SHOOK PAKISTAN AND INDIA, LEAVING DEVASTATION IN ITS WAKE. When the bodies were counted there were over 80,000 dead and almost 3,000,000 were homeless.

That same day, US Ambassador to Pakistan, Ryan C. Crocker, announced that the US would provide $500,000 in emergency aid to assist the communities affected by the earthquake. In his announcement he made this statement: "We offer our deepest sympathy to those affected by the earthquake and the families of the victims. We remain deeply concerned for all affected by this disaster." This was just the beginning of the assistance from the US forces; they would send food, medical supplies, and other forms of relief to the people of Pakistan.

Just a few days after the earthquake, the US began deploying the 212th Mobile Army Surgical Hospital (MASH) to help aid in the medical needs of the survivors and distribute vaccinations for those in need of them.

When the earthquake first occurred, I wanted to go to Pakistan, but because this was during the time that my dad was extremely sick, BT felt that I needed to stay where I was in the event I had to get home quickly if my dad took a turn for the worse. Looking back, I am grateful that I didn't go to Pakistan right away, because I was able to have the chance to say goodbye to my dad and attend his funeral. That may not have happened had I left for Pakistan any sooner.

BT sent some people to Pakistan without even having a contract. BT is a businessman through and through, and he heard that even though other large government contractors were supposed to support the relief mission, it turned out that they never did actually follow through. BT knew if we were there and in place when the military found themselves in need of supplies that it would be easier to get the contracts.

He sent a team of about ten people to make contact with a contracting officer; when it was determined that the other contractors would not be supporting the troops in this mission, our company began work.

Our job was troop life support, which meant we

basically covered all of their living needs: food, bottled water, port-a-johns, power generation, shower units, and most anything else that they might need to just get through the day.

The man BT had in charge of the Pakistan job was not doing very well. There were still no contracts signed or paper trails of any kind, and this was not good for our business if the military decided not to pay us. The military does everything with paperwork; if there is no paperwork, there is no contract. Ask any soldier who has ever had paperwork issues when it comes to their pay – nothing happens until the ink is put to the bottom line and then copied in triplicate. It is no different for the contractors that work with the military; we all know to make sure the contracts are signed and sent through the proper channels or nobody will get paid. With or without the contracts signed, we still had to pay our workers and incur the purchase and shipping charges. Our suppliers would not care if we were paid or not, they would expect to be paid on time. After my dad passed away, I needed something to keep my mind occupied to keep me from drowning in the grief, so BT said it was time for me to go in and take care of business.

DARE, DREAM, DISCOVER

The first thing I had to do was get in there and get those contracts signed. We had already shipped in over a million dollars in supplies such as food without a contract. I couldn't believe anyone would be so lax as to allow such a thing to happen.

This was my first order of business, but I would discover quickly that there was a great deal to clean up once I had the contracts in hand. I would find myself taking care of a flooded kitchen, downed generators, and of course sending a few people home who had not done their job. It is never a task to enjoy when I have to let someone go, but in this case I was just relieved to have them out of there so I could focus on doing my job and getting things in some kind of order again.

The MASH unit was doing a lot of good, but there was so much pain and sadness in Pakistan due to the devastating effects of the earthquake. Right after I arrived, I met a little girl in the tent hospital who had lost almost all of her family in the earthquake. To look at her, one would have thought she was a burn victim because of the condition of her young body. She couldn't have been more than seven or eight years old, and there she was with her skin peeled off from a large portion of her body. She looked like the saddest little girl in the world; she was crying her heart out to the point that I thought my own heart would break. The contracting officer there with me had some candy. It's funny how something as minor as a piece of candy can calm a child down. It didn't make her look any happier, but the candy he gave her made her stop crying. As we left, they started to scrub the debris out of her skin again, and she started screaming louder. From there we barely walked around the corner before we saw a baby hooked up to monitors. She had been born prematurely and survived.

The parents stood over their child, so grateful that their daughter had made it into this world, even under the worst of circumstances. I would later find out that this was the first baby born in the MASH unit in Pakistan. I felt like I was on an emotional roller coaster most of the time because of all of the things happening all at once. It was hard for anyone there to not realize just how precious and fragile life was, and often we were reminded of the strength of the human spirit.

Not everything about my job was quite so stressful. In fact, there were some things that gave me lots of joy that no amount of money or jewelry could ever bring. We had a project that we called Operation Teddy Bear. As Christmas drew near, I was in a meeting with the contracting officers. As we were planning the Christmas dinner and the events for that day, someone asked if we also wanted to do something for the children.

Someone said they wanted to do something really special and asked if anyone had any ideas. I told them I had been involved with Operation Teddy Bear the year before in Iraq and suggested that we do something similar in Pakistan. I told them that our company could donate teddy bears and t-shirts for the children. That started the ball rolling. Quickly everyone jumped in with getting other companies to donate toys, teddy bears, and candy.

We had sent Christmas trees to all of the base camps before Christmas, and on Christmas Day the base camps were open to the general public. As the civilian population came in, it was our chance to play Santa Claus. I flew with a general and some other contracting officers to each of the camps with garbage bags full of toys and gifts for the children. While I often missed my own family for the holidays, there is no greater joy in the world for me than to watch the faces of these children, who had nothing, receive their gifts; their smiling faces will stay with me forever. BT pointed something out that I hadn't even realized at the time: the parents were smiling. He told me that it's always great to make a child smile, but when something you do also makes their parents smile, then you have done something really special.

Who wouldn't want to give any child a Christmas gift? Who wouldn't want to bring a little bit of joy to people who had been devastated by something as horrific as an earthquake? To me, it was just human nature, it was a very small thing in the scheme of things, and I still wonder who really got more joy out of that day: the children of Pakistan, or those of us who were able to bring a smile to the faces of the people there. I had seen so much pain and misery since arriving in Pakistan that it was a gift for me to actually have a moment of joy.

The troops were amazing, and it became my pleasure to help bring in and set up their holiday meals. We had Thanksgiving, Christmas, and New Years meals for them. To watch these troops so far from their home and family during these very family-oriented holidays made me sad for them. We wanted to offer something special for the holidays, so we went all out and decorated the mess areas with all the things one might find at home, such as lights and a Christmas tree. Of course dinner had to be a traditional holiday meal with all of the trimmings. It didn't seem like much to us, but to the troops it was a touch of the homes they missed so much, and I hope in some small way we were able to show them how much they were truly appreciated.

I stayed in a house not far from the base, and sometimes in a nearby hotel; in both of these places I experienced the aftershock tremors of the earthquake. I don't think I was ever as scared during any job as I was during these tremors. Both times I was awakened by the bed shaking and vibrating. My first instinct was to run outside because I was afraid the walls and roof would come crashing in on me. Luckily they didn't, but the pool at the hotel ended up with a huge crack from the tremor. The entire experience seemed terrible to me at that time, and I could not even begin to grasp what the actual earthquake had to be like, as I was told that the tremors were nothing compared to the real thing. I was glad that I didn't have to find out what it was like to live through an earthquake.

PAKISTAN

Pakistan is not a rich country; even before the earthquake it was the epitome of a third world country. People drive in ways I have never seen. There seem to be no traffic laws and no thought or consideration for pedestrians. One of the first things I saw upon arriving in Pakistan was a man step in front of a car. The car was moving so fast that it actually tossed him in the air upon impact. As shocking as this was for me, it seemed to be nothing out of the ordinary for the locals.

I was saddened to see people literally crawling and begging for money. I had seen begging in Kosovo, but this place was so much worse. What broke my heart the most was the begging children. They were in the streets begging, and I so wanted to just give them money, but when I said something to one of the partners from our company, he told me that was the worst thing I could do. He explained that giving the kids money was not helping the children, but supporting the terrorists.

It broke my heart to hear how the money never went to the kids, but instead they were abused and used to get the money. If the children don't bring enough money home, they are often beaten, starved, and sometimes even have their fingers cut off for failing to bring in enough. Our partner explained that he gave money to charities that were set up specifically to help the children through education and other means of support.

Some women are treated horribly in Pakistan. Similar to the treatment that women suffer in Afghanistan, the women of Pakistan are abused terribly. Before I continue with this, I would like to make very clear that not all women are treated badly. Many are loved, adored, and spoiled by their husbands, just as is true in places such as Kuwait. I have traveled many places in my life, but none made me as sad as Pakistan did.

I could see that once the earthquake crisis was over, most people would forget about it, and the Pakistanis would still be there starving with little hope of a better life and suffering at the hands of abusers. It saddens me to see anyone mistreated, but the level of torture the people of Pakistan suffer is heartbreaking. Even during my childhood when my mother would leave me with nothing, I always had people I could go to if I really needed help, but the Pakistanis have no one to help them and often those who try to help them end up dead.

More and more attention is being brought to the

women's movement in Pakistan. I am not saying that all women are abused or oppressed, but for those who are abused in Pakistan, there is a movement that is starting to draw attention from the rest of the world.

One woman, Mukhtar Mai, has dedicated her life to the plight of Pakistani women. Her goal is to bring more education to the women, wipe out illiteracy and give them a fighting chance for a better life. She has spoken to world leaders and anyone else who might listen or help in making life better for Pakistani women. Her journey began in 2002 when she was gang-raped on orders of a village council to pay for the crimes of her brother. After testifying against her assailants in court, she was given a monetary compensation; instead of spending that money on herself, she used it to build schools and start a shelter for abused women. Named Woman of the Year in 2005 by Glamour magazine, she continues her fight today.

Another brave woman who had been a great champion of the Pakistani women lost her life recently. Zille Huma Usman, the wife of a doctor and was also the Punjab Minister for Social Welfare. She was a fine example of the ability of a Pakistani woman–she was the first woman to hold any office within the government–and she was a symbol of change and hope for all of the women of Pakistan. She proved to all of Pakistan that a woman could do the job and do it well. Sadly, in February of 2007, Muhammad Sarwar made the choice to disagree that she had the right to work, and a woman holding a government office was even more distasteful to him.

He walked up to her in a crowd stating that women do not have the right to work and shot her in the face. She was flown to a nearby hospital, but surgery and all the efforts of the doctors proved to be futile.

Zille Huma Usman died in the prime of her life in a place that she had hoped to make better for everyone. Her killer would tell the police that he felt no remorse for his crime. He would later be sentenced to death for her murder, but it will be difficult to find another woman to fill her shoes.

The bravery and courage of these women in the worst of circumstances has inspired many women to try to do what they say can't be done. I can only pray that the dreams of both women will not end in death or defeat; instead I hope more people will be inspired to join their fight and make not only Pakistan but the world a better place for all people–both men and women. Our children need heroes, and people such as Mukhtar Mai and Zille Huma Usman are true heroes; they have made the world a better place by their actions. If we can teach our children that this kind of accomplishment is what true heroes are made of, then I believe we can have a world with peace, compassion and understanding.

The 212th would leave Pakistan in 2006; they had been the last MASH unit left, and now they have disbanded. While many people didn't give Pakistan a second thought, it was a historic event for the US Army as they brought in their tent hospitals and medical treatment to people who would otherwise have been left to die in the streets.

For me it was reminder of how blessed I am and how much I really have in this life. It also reinforced my desire to make this world a better place for others. I so badly wanted to help the women and children of Pakistan, but I could only go in and do my job. Any money I might have given them would not have gone to help them, which seemed like such an insane concept to me.

I left Pakistan with a prayer that someday these people would know a better life, a life with enough food and shelter, and without fear. I don't know if that will ever happen, but I hope that others will take notice and do something to help them before it's too late.

I do want to make it very clear that the atrocities described here are not a reflection on all Pakistani people. For the most part, Pakistan is an absolutely beautiful country and has wonderful people. Most families are just doing the best they can to survive; the men love their wives and children, just like with families all over the world.

Just as many judge groups of people by faith, race, or gender, the people of Pakistan are often judged by the few who don't want a country that is a thriving, safe, and peaceful place. I don't and never have supported terrorism; I support the people who are victimized by a minority who make it hard for Pakistanis to have a decent and safe life.

I still work with many Pakistani people who are very decent and very hard-working. I have many friends from Pakistan. These are people just like you and me; all they want is a better life for themselves and their families. So, when I speak of the bad things in Pakistan, I truly hope you can be open-minded and look at the entire picture instead of just the select few that make life very difficult for the rest.

When I began blogging, it was therapy for me. This is one of the entries from my blog when I was trying to get across to people that someone is not a terrorist just because they come from a certain part of the world or a certain faith:

Am I a Terrorist? Do I Support Terrorism?

In reading some of the blogs posted on this site, it would seem that I support terrorism if I do not condemn all Muslims for their beliefs.

For the record: I'm not a terrorist and I do not support terrorism.

A little history about me: I spent 11 years at Eglin Air Force Base. I supported the US Government in Kosovo for over a year. I was in Iraq for 6 months. I was in Kuwait for over 2 years, and am now living in Dubai. All this time I have supported the US government in some type of form or fashion.

I am strongly against terrorism, terrorist movements, and any groups that support and encourage terrorism. I feel the same about dictators like Saddam Hussein. I do not want to see another holocaust-type event in my lifetime. I already had to deal with experiencing first hand what Milosevic's actions did in Kosovo. I felt the pain, death, and destruction of the Albanian people while I was there. I saw pictures of Kurdish children that were killed by chemical weapons at the hand of Saddam Hussein. Mass grave are a devastating site to me.

I believe in the security and safety of the US first and foremost. I believe and support the US in actions taken in securing the freedom and safety for US citizens, including our war on terrorism.

Does that mean I'm not allowed to be a compassionate person? No! I know there are innocent lives lost in war, and that will always make me sad. I don't care how much the bad guys deserve to get blown to smithereens, I will always care and be compassionate about the innocent lives lost, just as much as I cared and will always hold sorrow in my heart for the innocent victims, civilians, fire department and police force that lost their lives in 9/11. I was in a fire department for 11 years. It felt like half my family died in one day when the towers went down. I can't even explain the grief and sorrow I felt in my heart. When I visited the Anne Frank house in Amsterdam ... I can't even describe what felt like physical pain in my heart, not just sadness. Seeing things close up like that makes it more intense ... just as I have witnessed things first hand away from the US.

Do I think all Serbians should burn in hell for what happened to the people of Albania? No. Do I think that all Albanians are innocent and good and do not have organized crime and bad political groups? I know better!

I have and always will refuse to believe that all Muslims are bad and are taught to hate all Americans and that they are taught that we are their worst enemy. I know that some sects teach this and that is bad.

I have lived among Muslims from different countries for over 4 years now. I have been

DARE, DREAM, DISCOVER

welcomed into their homes. I have worked for and with Muslims. Over the thousands that I have come in contact with, I will say that they are the kindest and most tolerant religion I have ever experienced. Never once was I told by a Muslim that I would burn in hell or that I needed to convert to their beliefs. I can honestly say out of the thousands with whom I've had conversations, had dinner in their homes, and worked around, I have never been confronted about converting to their religion. I have never been persuaded to listen to their opinions or their views on Islam, Christianity, or any type of religious opinion or personal opinion they have towards Americans.

To view or consider all Muslims as hating and despising all Americans is a purely ignorant statement. If that were true, the Muslims that I have been exposed to sure have put on a good show of hospitality, acceptance, and a pure love for humanity in general. And I will always be thankful to the Muslim man that put me and my sister on a plane from Kuwait to the US when my father was on his death bed. I will also be thankful to the office staff

222

of Muslims that sent dozens of flowers to my father when he was sick and to his funeral. That meant a lot to me and my non-Muslim family.

I would like to recognize and thank the Muslim staff in Kuwait that supported over 350 million dollars worth of supplies and services delivered to the US troops in Iraq and Afghanistan last year.

This is all unlike my experience in the US with being exposed to several different religions, where I experienced people that were judgmental and confrontational and was told several times that if I did not convert to their religion, I would go to hell.

One of my sisters to this day thinks that I'm going to hell because I do not read the King James Version of the Bible. But do I stereotype all Christians? No! Do I believe all Christians think I'm going to hell? No! But, frankly, I do not care what other Christians or other people think of me or my views.

I have proudly served my country, and I proudly serve a God that I try to honor and respect by accepting and loving people and accepting different cultures as He does. That even means the ignorant people who have not been exposed to the reality of different cultures and REAL PEOPLE of this world, or who simply do not know any better than to try to shove their views and opinions down people's throats on daily basis.

Yes, everyone is entitled to their opinion. I can accept and respect that, but I do not always agree.

CHAPTER XIV

DUBAI

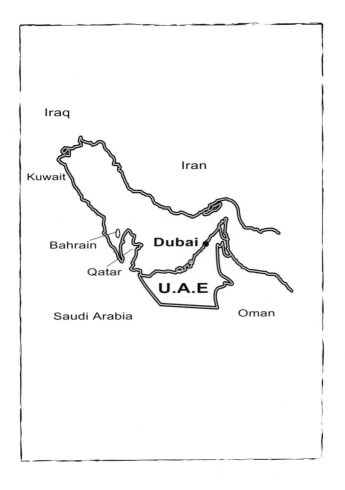

DUBAI HAS THE LARGEST POPULATION IN THE UNITED ARAB EMIRATES AND IS BUILT FOR TOURISM AND HIGH COMMERCE. If one were to compare Dubai to a city in the United States, it would probably be a cross between Las Vegas, Beverly Hills, and New York City, but it is impossible to imagine what Dubai is really like unless you have been there.

There is evidence that implies that Dubai dates back to before Christ, although there is little to be found in the history books to know exactly when Dubai was founded and settled. More recent history of Dubai tells of a fishing village in the 18th century and began to expand in population when the Al Bu Falasa tribe arrived during the 19th century. As well as being fishermen, they also worked in the pearl and marine trade to earn a living and begin building what is now Dubai.

Over the next 100 years, the economy of Dubai began to grow as settlers came in from India, Pakistan, and Iran. With the growth in population also came the growth of

DARE, DREAM, DISCOVER

Dubai and its economic system. Today many make Dubai their weekend or holiday getaway and a place to go and have some fun during their vacation. For me Dubai held a promise of independence, a company that I could run, and a way to start with a clean slate.

BT knew I was serious when I told him that I had purchased a condo in the Dominican Republic. I wanted out from our relationship and from the heartbreak he was causing me every single day. I had fallen head over heels in love with him. I had loved others before him and, looking back, I realize they were probably not much more than a girl looking for love and accepting what she thought love felt like. With BT, I was in love to the point that I couldn't do much else except think about him and want to be with him. I wanted a life with him, but I knew that would never be possible because he would never be willing to give that to me.

I didn't want for anything in the material sense, but money could not buy the one thing that I wanted most: the love and security of a life and family with BT. It was and is the only thing he has ever denied me. Sadly, it is really the only thing that I wanted from him. I loved him

228

with all that I had, and I believe he loves me as much as he is capable of loving any one person, but I doubt he will ever love anyone enough to give up all of his other women. I was starting to hate myself because of the way he was treating me. I once told him that he made me feel like an insect being tortured by a cat. Instead of killing it all at once and putting it out of it's misery, a cat will often tear its victim apart little piece by little piece, imparting a slow and treacherous death upon its prey. I was being tortured slowly and it was killing me inside.

I had to make a clean break, and I had to make it fast before I fell any harder or lost my nerve to leave. BT knew I was serious about leaving, and he was very serious about keeping me near him. He even went as far as purchasing a property in the Dominican Republic next to mine just to keep me near, but for the time being he came up with a different plan for me.

He was starting up a company in Dubai. He knew I loved it there, and I suppose that was his way of dangling a carrot on a stick in front of me to convince me to continue to work with him. I was made a managing partner in this new investment property company and would be responsible for getting it up and running. How could I turn this down? I would have a company to get going from the ground up in a place that I loved. I had to get a license to sell real estate in Dubai and while there is paperwork to do in order to get that, you don't have to take a test. So, I did the paperwork, paid my fee, and I was set to do business in Dubai. We would have several branches all over the world, including one in the Dominican Republic. It was up to me to get people hired, trained, find clients, set up the website, and take care of any other details large or small.

No matter what kind of personal relationship we had, BT had confidence in my skills as a businessperson. I had dreams in the back of my head that I would be the female Donald Trump of the Middle East and once again BT would get what he wanted: me.

Of course, now there was even more reason for us to be in constant contact with one another, and somehow without realizing what I had done, I had given BT complete control over my life. For BT it was a win-win situation; he had everything he wanted. He wouldn't lose me as long as I was running this company and, of course, that put him in my life constantly. He wouldn't have to let me go, and in the meantime he would add a new company to his list of many successes in his own life. For me it was the chance of a lifetime: I was starting a property investment company that would be the first US-based company in Dubai of its kind. I thrived on the thrill and the excitement of it all; I imagined excelling beyond even the imagination of the Donald Trumps of the world.

Dubai would also be the beginning of a long and deep depression for me. Just because I had told BT I was done with our romantic relationship did not mean that he accepted that from me. I had been with other men in my life, even loved them on some level, but none came close to what I felt for BT, and he knew how to pull every last ounce of resistance I had.

When I first arrived in Dubai I was living in a condominium, but it was a temporary situation, so I didn't bother to unpack. It was rather like a hotel stay. I lived out of a suitcase and had no internet, cable, or even a car to connect me to the rest of world. I was alone and horribly lonely in a new city. I began to write as a form of therapy; the lonelier I became, the more I wrote.

DARE, DREAM, DISCOVER

I had always considered writing a book about my life to tell others that, no matter how bad their background might be, they could have it all if they really wanted to go out and get it, but I was also beginning to see that I didn't have it all. I had the possessions, but I didn't have the joy and the happiness that is often associated with those things. Instead, I found myself feeling as I did in my childhood, empty and alone.

What did it matter if I could go buy anything I wanted if I was alone and hurting over a man who thought I was behaving like a "typical female"? Since when did wanting love and a family have to be exclusively a female emotion? I knew there were men out there who wanted the same things – too bad I hadn't fallen in love with one of them. I had learned at a young age to keep myself distanced from anyone that could really hurt me.

My mother and step-father had taught me that trusting or loving someone too much would only hurt me in the end, and my years in the fire department helped me perfect the skill of self-protection. I was strong and independent. I never allowed myself to fall too hard for anyone or let anyone close enough to know the real me: the me that could be hurt, the me that was vulnerable, the me that wanted to love and be loved in return. I had my life under control and I was indestructible until I met BT. The two men I had ever truly loved in my lifetime were gone now. My father had passed away, and while BT was most definitely living and breathing, he was as unreachable as my dad was at this point. He wanted me to jump when he decided to make the time for me, but all I got in return was being his trophy date at parties full of prostitutes. I wanted and deserved better than that, but I was like a moth to a flame where he was concerned.

All BT had to do was call, and for a minute or two he would act like we still had a romantic relationship. Each time my heart leapt into my throat as I prayed that maybe he might finally realize how much I loved and needed him and would decide that he couldn't live without me. Of course, each time I was crushed as he toyed with my heart.

He might have been my prince–and I lived like a princess in many ways–but I was treated no better than a pauper who came begging at his door.

Little by little I began to break away from him as the pain went from the intense soul-crushing misery to a dull ache that never really went away. It wasn't so bad, kind of like a nagging backache that you eventually just become used to and learn to live with.

I finally moved into my own place. I found a nice little community where I lived in a townhouse with all the amenities. In many ways it is set up like a small, private town; if I didn't want to leave the gates of my community ever again, I really wouldn't have to, because it has everything: restaurants, a golf course, equestrian center, grocery store, travel agency, dry cleaner, nail studio, hair salon/spa, and even a liquor store!

My townhouse is equipped with a tanning bed and a hair salon. It's a dream home for many, but for me it's like a prison. It was months and months before I quit living out of suitcases and boxes and actually made an effort to move in. It might have been home, but it was an empty and lonely home.

After I finally got my internet access and other basics, I was searching the web when I ran across a site for bloggers that was a bit different than some of the others. It claimed to be a place for writers. While I never considered myself a professional writer, I thought I might find someone to help me with my book there. I decided to join and begin to tell my story.

I wondered if anyone would really be interested in my story. I have to admit I was a little surprised by the reception that I received from what seemed to be a rather tight-knit community of people. I was amazed by the diversity of the group and how many of them seemed to come to read what I was writing. Many reached out to me and offered support and kindness; some were not so kind and called me a gold-digger who got what she deserved; others seemed to be able to identify with parts of my story.

I felt like I had found a home in ways with this group of people. We had all the things that families have: we supported one another, cheered when something good happened to one of us, felt sad when something bad happened and oh yes, we even disagreed on just about anything you can think to disagree on.

For me, what really troubled and upset me the most was when there seemed to be a crusade to attack Muslims as a whole. I tried to explain to them, I tried to help them understand that what had been put out in the media was not always true. Many complained about the media's coverage of the conflict in Iraq and how they didn't tell the truth, but these same people were convinced that everything bad that had ever been published about the Muslims in the news must be true. I couldn't understand how normal rational, kind, and compassionate people could be so blind and so hateful toward any one group.

Most of these attackers claimed to be devout Christians. I was stunned; I am a Christian and I was never taught that hating or persecuting anyone was in God's plan. It seemed the more I tried to explain to them that they were only hearing about the radicals, the more determined they were to prove me wrong. They seemed to have forgotten that I served with great pride in the US Air Force. They forgot that 9/11 touched me deeply. I watched the buildings implode with what felt like my family inside; we lost several hundred firefighters that day, and those were my brothers and sisters in uniform.

It was the country that I had served so proudly that had been attacked by some of the most evil people on earth; the fact that they were Muslim made them no less or no more evil than Hitler or anyone else who has ever murdered people out of hatred. I was so disappointed in my fellow countrymen and saddened by their closed minds. I realized that there was little I could do to change their hatred toward Muslims because of the actions of a very select few.

I know of soldiers who have lost brothers and sisters in uniform at the hands of terrorists who are much more tolerant of the differences, yet the people that claim to support these men and women were writing things that went against everything an American soldier stands for.

When did they forget that democracy means freedom for all faiths, races, genders, and creeds? I suppose I will never understand how one can hate another simply based on an opinion as opposed to getting the facts.

When the conflict between Israel and Lebanon came to a head, I was horrified. The news here showed some very graphic footage. It started to really affect me in a way that probably wasn't good for me, but as I watched the news and saw dead children and innocent civilians who had no real way to escape, I found myself becoming more and more upset by the situation. It seemed as if I cried every single day of this conflict, and what really bothered me was to hear people say that the people who died should have evacuated. These people didn't have the luxury of getting in their car and going somewhere else. Most were on foot; how far can a person get that way? Those who did evacuate were put into shelters that were also bombed. An entire building in the city of Qana collapsed during an air strike, trapping and killing those who were there for shelter.

Out of the 50 people who died in that building, 37 were children. How do we consider that any kind of victory for anyone? To whom did those children pose a threat? How was it that the Christians of the world missed the fact that the people in Lebanon were also Christian? I guess they forgot that in all of their self-righteous indignation against Lebanon.

The situation between the two countries is very tense– I know that and I understand that it has been going on for many years–but neither side is more right or more wrong than the other. Innocent people who have nothing to do with the conflict are dying on both sides. Didn't we become upset about 9/11 because innocent civilians were attacked? What makes Lebanon and its innocent civilians any different? I found myself realizing that some people simply like to pick sides and claim one is for good and the other is evil; what I saw in this conflict was dead children and women who wanted nothing more than to stay safe in this mess.

On a more positive note, I was able to find someone in the blog group to help me write my book. I am not sure what drew us to one another, but we quickly found that we had a great deal in common.

Her husband was recently home from a tour in Iraq, and we discovered that my sister Nickie was working at the very same base camp at the same time that her husband had been there. We also discovered that we had similar backgrounds, and it just felt right to ask her to help me write my book.

I also tried to show the people in the blog group a bit of Dubai from afar. I can only touch on a small portion of what Dubai is like and the energy that resonates here. It's a huge commerce area, a great tourist attraction, and a very family-oriented area. I have said many times that I would not hesitate to raise my children here because of the emphasis put on family and values.

Women don't walk around in Daisy Dukes, nor do you see their breasts or other body parts hanging out as they walk down the street. I am able to get a good deal of American TV here, and it makes me sad when the news seems to focus on people such as Britney Spears or Anna Nicole Smith. I don't think that if I had a daughter I would want her to think that either of these women were examples to be followed. We watch the Hollywood news shows today to discover Anna Nicole was stoned on something during her pregnancy, and Britney Spears is out running around partying while she is in a custody battle. Is this really the image we want our daughters to follow?

Here in Dubai, modesty and respect are extremely important to everyone; not even the tourists walk around in skimpy clothing. When we talk about respect for women between the Middle East and the Western world, I find myself wondering which society really respects women more.

I am finding that the American dream that I grew up hearing about is not really so achievable in America anymore. I hear my friends and family talk about an economy that is failing, record-high foreclosure rates, and unemployment that is through the roof. Poverty is apparently no longer something for the few, as more companies leave the US to go to other countries where they don't pay half of their profit in taxes.

The current ruler of Dubai, His Highness Sheikh Mohammed bin Rashid Al Maktoum, is a visionary in many ways. His vision did not begin with him but with his father, who wanted Dubai to be more than a fishing village that someday would die out and become another poverty-stricken area of the world. He knows, as did his father, that eventually the oil money will run out.

They want Dubai to be prepared to continue to compete on the world market and become a Mecca for economic growth. With their creative and innovative ideas, Dubai is now becoming the world's marketplace for business both big and small.

Bringing Dubai into the 21st century has meant including internet technology and e-business, and utilizing all of the most up-to-date and innovative technological developments of our time to bring in more business and make doing business in Dubai easier. Dubai Internet City and Dubai Media City were put into place to ensure that the majority of the world's big business players could have a presence in Dubai. Internet City is a project development with several high-rise buildings.

There are various companies that conduct business in offices there. Media City is close by and has business offices for CNN, BBC, and Showtime to name a few. Media City also has a lot of PR and advertising firms. Also close is a development called Knowledge Village, where you can take various learning courses, including foreign language studies, on-line trading, and hypnotherapy.

The vision of His Highness Sheikh Mohammed bin Rashid Al Maktoum has become more than a dream in Dubai; it has become a reality. When I look around Dubai, this is what I imagined the American dream to look like: a place where dreams do come true if you are willing to work for them. Dubai does all it can to make it possible for these businesses to get off of the ground and thrive.

All one has to do is look around at the business players that are here or looking here to set up at least a branch of their business. Donald Trump is developing The Palm Trump International Hotel & Tower, a 600-million dollar, five-star hotel and is developing other real estate projects here. Tiger Woods has also discovered the advantages of doing business in Dubai, choosing Dubai as the site for his very first golf course. Scheduled to open in 2009 in Dubailand, the largest tourism and commerce project in Dubai, it will not be just any golf course, but will include a 6000 square foot clubhouse, 320 mansions and villas, and a golf academy.

In an interview with USA Today upon the announcement of his development plans, Tiger Woods stated: "I have been amazed by the progress of Dubai. From the time I first came to play here in 2000, I wanted to be a part of this amazing vision."

Dubai is also the home of the only seven-star hotel in the world: The Burj Al Arab. It is built to resemble a billowing sail along the Dubai coastline. Naomi Campbell liked this hotel so much that she rented 15 floors for a week recently as a birthday gift to herself.

At night it is a sight to behold with sculptures of colored water and fire. This is a place to drive by and see even if you don't stay there, but if you are staying there, make sure that you take a ride in the chauffer-driven Rolls Royce they provide so you can see how beautiful it is at night.

Dubai became one of my favorite places in the world from the very first time I visited BT. Now I was living in

DARE, DREAM, DISCOVER

Dubai with all of the luxuries and excitement, and yet I wasn't happy. I loved the real estate work I was doing, but my heart was always with the troops. I never entirely stopped working with government contracting, and that was still what made me the happiest when it came to work. I loved the development company, I loved what I accomplished, but I loved the feeling of helping the troops more than anything I had ever done in my life.

I found my heart drawing me back to it again and again. Finally, I took a business trip back to Iraq and ended up staying for two months. I realized that the base camps still needed support and my heart had never left them, no matter where I was living or what kind of work I was doing. It was time to begin a new venture.

I finally made the emotional break from BT and made it clear that, although I would do business with him, I would no longer be his girlfriend. He admitted to being emotionally dependent on me and even threatened to shut down the investment property company if I left. Again, he was emotionally blackmailing me. So, I wouldn't leave the investment property business; I would turn it over to others to run. After all, it is my company – I built it, I helped it grow, and a large part of my heart will always be there–but like a parent letting go with a child, the time had come that the business could do just fine without me there every minute of the day. I wanted to go back to government contracting, so that is just what I did.

I had been working with a company that handled government contracting all along, but I had put it on the back burner while I got my investment property company off the ground. Other people were running it and doing a good job, but now it was time for me to go back to where my heart had always been. I went back and found that I once again felt I was doing something good.

Today, that is what I am still doing and I love every crazy minute of it. I love watching the result as we get much-needed supplies to the base camps, I love knowing that what I am doing is truly making life better and helping the troops. I have found my place in my career, now I just have to find a way to apply that to my personal life.

*   *   *

This is something that I wrote shortly after I made the final emotional break with BT:

DARE, DREAM, DISCOVER

Getting Over the Hardest Breakup in My Life

I thought at first that I would not be able to live, feel, breathe, and be the same person that I was before I met you, or be like the carefree person that I was at the beginning of our relationship. I was still childlike and a dreamer full of life and ambition.

I can't describe this pain in words. The pain you have caused me. This pain is from the deepest pit of my stomach.

The tears were so heavy and full of grief. I did not want to function; I did not want to leave my bed or my house. I felt paralyzed knowing that I had to cut you out of my life. It is so hard to let people into my life anyway ... I will never forget how that feeling of abandonment and betrayal first felt when my mother abandoned me the first time ... I was left with my step-father and half-sister.

I didn't know what happened to my mother; was she murdered? It was 5 days before the police found her car at a truck stop with a note attached to her car saying how her family is better off without her (um...excuse me, but that meant me!). She ran off with another one of her boyfriend flings. I hate letting people in my life only later to be betrayed or abandoned. But, slowly the pain has eased up ... it is like a slow, gratifying graduation of the pain level ever so slowly going down a notch or two every few days or weeks. I can just visualize an image of the needle all the way in the red at level ten for the worst pain and then slowly moving into the green months later at level 3. The thing that makes it the hardest is when you call and act like we still have a relationship, and for 1 or 2 minutes I play along only to be reminded quickly, oh so quickly, how you have hurt me and lied to me and will continue to do so every time I give you the opportunity.

So it is pain again, but it does get easier each time. I know 100% that I will find the right person or at least someone who respects me and respects my feelings. I have succeeded in everything at life so far that I have diligently worked for, I've always felt like I've deserved the best, and I've felt that I should be paid and compensated for how hard I work and the business that I bring in, and I have accomplished that.

DARE, DREAM, DISCOVER

Why should I settle for anything less in a personal relationship? I have made more in one month than I did in a year's work with my previous jobs in the US when I was younger. I know that dreams come true and I can have it all. I want love, but more than that, I want the respect of the person that loves me ... it seems like the two (love & respect) would go hand in hand, but it did not with you.

Anyway, it is a good feeling to know that I'm strong enough to take back my life and not let you control it in an ugly way. You make me think back to when my mother used to tell me that I wasn't good enough to have the person that I wanted to be with. I had the biggest crush on this guy and she told me..."you are not good enough for him." In your world, I should be happy to have someone like you ... you lie and cheat on me, but you tell me that I'm the most important thing in your life.

You take care of me in monetary ways. You tell me that there is no such thing as a perfect relationship and that I should not be concerned with having children and a family, that I should be focused on my career and that I shouldn't get "emotional."

You tell me how I'm being a "typical female".

You make it sound so bad to dream about having someone by my side to share my life with.

I know now beyond a shadow of a doubt that I am good enough to deserve those things and I will have those things. Just because you want to live a life of lies and deceit doesn't mean I want to. Just because you can't be happy and content with one person and not have to fool around all of the time, doesn't mean that I have to live my life that way.

You can't decide for me. You can't control my feelings. I know what I want and what I need in my life. You have no right and no power over me, my thoughts, my emotions, and my decisions. I will be a better person from this experience and I will appreciate love and appreciate family and friends and honesty more than ever before.

Thank you for that valuable lesson ... you have reminded me what really matters in life. Good luck to you, I wish the best for you, and I will always look at our relationship in a positive way because every experience in my life, including our relationship, has made me the person that I am today and I'm proud of that. That was one thing that my father told me before he passed away, that one reason that he was content in his short life was because he was proud of his children.

I will never forget looking into his beautiful blue eyes and seeing such love, pride, and admiration for me. That meant a lot coming from my dad. He was never the affectionate type or one to communicate very well. We always had a stand-offish relationship before he got really sick.

I've had the greatest teachers in life ... sometimes they are my estranged parents, sometimes they are my best friend, sometimes they are my boss, and, yes, sometimes they are the men in my gone-south relationship. But, if I could have a Hollywood-type romance/ Business Mogul/ Billionaire of a man in a relationship, B.T. was it. No one will ever come close on that front ... nor would I ever want that again. It was one of the greatest chapters of all in my life. Thank you B.T., no matter what, you will always be my special prince ... I will love you forever ... your name and memories are branded very deep into my heart, veins, and soul.

*   *   *

I wrote this after seeing one particular baby in the Gulf Newspaper after he was killed in the Qana air strike against Lebanon in 2006:

To the Innocent Children of Lebanon: I'm sorry that I killed you.

Dear Baby Abbas,

Since my country and I are for the war on terrorism, I feel responsible for your death. My country did not call a cease-fire because of what Hezbollah stands for.

Baby Abbas, you were in Qana when they bombed you. You were not supposed to be there. I know you were only nine months olds. How can anyone hold you responsible for not evacuating? How can anyone hold you responsible for reports that missiles were fired from your location to Israel? How can anyone hold you responsible for terrorism?

Baby Abbas, today you are known as the youngest victim of the bloodiest act that has happened so far in this war. I have seen the pictures of the other 12 corpses of babies that were huddled near you. Even though your stiff body is now covered with chalk and dust, I can see what a beautiful child you are. You were wearing green shorts and a teddy bear vest. The reports say that you had a peaceful look on your face like you were just sleeping. It is sad that you will never wake up. I pray that you rest in peace now and are frightened no more.

I pray for all of the innocent lives that are lost in this war. I know what it feels like to lose innocent lives in my country, too. I am told that this is the kind of pain that I have to accept and endure in order for my country to be and remain free. It is such a high price to pay.

To Baby Abbas and to all of the innocent victims who lose their lives and for the family members who have to suffer the loss of children, husbands, and other family members and loved ones in the name of freedom, I'm sorry and I feel guilty that it looks like my rights and my freedoms are more important than your rights, your life, and your freedoms. I believe that we are created by one God and he loves us all the same. Please know that I am suffering with your loss of life, I am grieving now, and a part of me has died because of this sad day.

I pray that, if nothing else, we can come together and agree as humans that it is wrong for innocent civilians to die in war and we should do everything in our power to ensure this does not happen. I don't think we can honestly say that we are doing this now. Gulf News in the UAE reports: "Before the bombings, Qana was a picturesque southern village of figs, grape vines and olive trees along rolling, rocky hills where Lebanese believe Jesus Christ turned water into wine for a wedding. It was here on April 18, 1996, when 106 people were killed when Israeli forces shelled a UN compound that had given refuge to 800 Lebanese. August 1, 2006."

*   *   *

DARE, DREAM, DISCOVER

My Closing Thoughts..........

Wars, rumors of wars, end times and heartache....all of this talk and all of this pain is a daily reality in my world. We all have difficult times and situations to make it through. Making it through is the key to survival.

If you can just look at the big picture and what is going on all over this great big world in general, I think it will help to minimize your own daily struggles.

I believe that by reaching out to help as many people as you can, you will find your own problems easier to deal with. That is what has worked for me and I hope that you will find peace on your journey by helping others. Maybe it is your next door neighbor that needs some encouragement today.

Reach out now! You will create a beautiful ripple effect by doing this that is so huge and so beautiful, you cannot even imagine the magnitude!

I sometimes find it hard to believe at the way my life has turned out. I am so glad that I broke out of the "normal way" of thinking and that I did not let my circumstances in life stop me from following my heart and dreams as a

254

little girl. Thanks to the encouragement and support of a few special people, it has really made a difference for me. Today, I can truly say that I am grateful for my life and every unique experience that I have been a part of.

So now I am challenging you to go for it! I dare you! I dare you to dream and I hope that you will discover the beauty and positive energy in people and in this world.

*   *   *

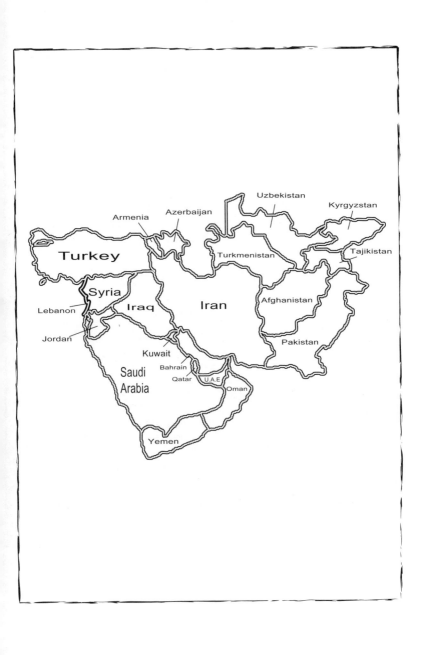

Hanging with
the Bradley
Crew On Camp
Speicher

Blerta's smile

Operation Teddy Bear In Pakistan

Pakistan Earthquake Moutain Slide Effect

First Iraqi Women
Hired on Camp
Speicher During
the War

Me Under the
Famous Crossed
Swords in Baghdad

Getting Ready
for my Flight

My Friend Alina who gave medical assistance to victims of
Pakistan Earthquake

Me, Relaxing waiting on a flight out of Iraq

Me and Sis

Me with the Major

I flew in General
Caseys Jet!

Serving Christmas Dinner to the US Troops in Pakistan

My Fire Crew that I assisted in Training in Kosovo, this was my
return visit to Blerta

Flying Over Baghdad